STEP - BY - STEP

ITALIAN

step-by-step

italian

Rosemary Wadey   Wendy Lee
Pamela Westland

This is a Parragon Publishing book

This edition published in 2001

Parragon Publishing
Queen Street House
4 Queen Street
Bath
BA1 1HE
UK

ISBN 0-75254-575-2

Printed in China

Cup measurements in this book are for American cups.
Tablespoons are assumed to be ½ fl oz.
Unless otherwise stated, milk is assumed to be full-fat,
eggs are medium, and pepper is freshly ground black pepper.

Contents

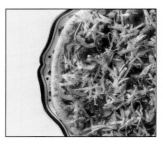

SIMPLE

Italian

RECIPES

With its exotic range of mouthwatering yet
healthy and nutritious dishes, Italian
cooking appeals to just about everyone. The
various regional cuisines all have something
special to offer, from quick and easy pasta
dishes to more ambitious delicacies such as
Saltimbocca and Tiramisu.

The warmth and vitality for which Italy is
renowned is reflected in the country's
cuisine, and this comprehensive book will
enable you to sample tasty dishes from all
over Italy. Over the following pages you will
find dishes with irresistible flavors and
aromas to tempt your taste buds and
encourage you to enter the wonderful
world of Italian cooking.

ANTIPASTI & SOUPS

•

PASTA & PIZZA

•

FISH & SHELLFISH

•

MEAT & POULTRY

•

DESSERTS

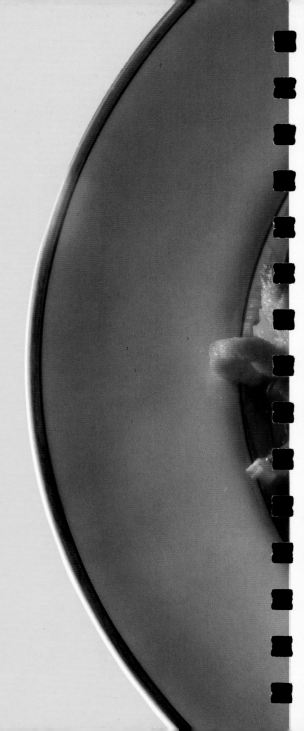

CHAPTER ONE

Antipasti & Soups

The word antipasto (plural antipasti) means "before the main course" and what is served may be simple and inexpensive or highly elaborate. Antipasti usually come in three categories: meat, fish, and vegetables. There are many varieties of cold meats, including ham, invariably sliced paper-thin. The best known is prosciutto from Parma, but there are many others, especially from the mountain areas, all of which can be served with slices of melon and figs. Numerous vegetables feature in antipasto dishes, served raw or marinated, deep-fried or pickled, with and without dressings. All varieties of fish are combined for the *antipasti di pesce*, including inkfish, octopus, and cuttlefish. Huge shrimp and mussels appear in various guises and fresh sardines are popular.

Soups too are a very important part of the Italian cuisine. They vary in consistency from very thin to virtually knife and fork soups. Minestrone is known world-wide, but the best-known version probably came from Milan; however, all kinds are full of vegetables, often with pasta or rice plus beans, and are delicious and satisfying. Fish soups abound in one guise or another, and most of these are village specialities, so the variety is unlimited. Many of these soups constitute a whole meal, particularly those with a large proportion of beans, or with lightly toasted slices of bread added to the bowl.

Opposite: *The Grand Canal, Venice. With its close proximity to the sea, fish and seafood dishes are found in abundance around Venice and the north-east corner of Italy.*

STEP 1

STEP 1

STEP 4

STEP 5

FISH SOUP

All over Italy the selection of fish is enormous. There are many varieties of fish soup, some including shellfish. You will find cream soups, thin soups, and thick soups: this one, from Tuscany, is like a chowder.

SERVES 4–6

2 lb assorted prepared fish (including mixed
  fish fillets, squid, etc.)
2 onions, sliced thinly
few sprigs fresh flat-leaf parsley
2 bay leaves
2 celery stalks, sliced thinly
²/₃ cup white wine
4¹/₂ cups water
2 tbsp olive oil
1 garlic clove, crushed
1 carrot, chopped finely
15-oz can peeled tomatoes, liquidized
2 potatoes, peeled and chopped
1 tbsp tomato paste
1 tsp freshly chopped oregano or ¹/₂ tsp
  dried oregano
2¹/₂ cups fresh mussels
1 cup peeled shrimp
2 tbsp chopped fresh parsley
salt and pepper
crusty bread, to serve

1 Cut the cleaned and prepared fish into slices or cubes and put into a large saucepan with 1 sliced onion, the parsley sprigs and bay leaves, 1 sliced celery stalk, the wine, and the water. Bring to a boil, cover, and simmer for about 25 minutes.

2 Strain the fish stock and discard the vegetables and herbs. Skin the fish, remove any bones, and reserve.

3 Heat the oil in a pan, finely chop the remaining onion, and fry with the garlic, carrot, and remaining celery until soft but not colored. Add the liquidized canned tomatoes, potatoes, tomato paste, oregano, reserved stock, and seasonings. Bring to a boil and simmer for about 15 minutes or until the potatoes are almost tender.

4 Meanwhile, thoroughly scrub the mussels. Add to the pan with the shrimp and simmer for about 5 minutes or until the mussels have opened (discard any that stay closed).

5 Add the fish to the soup with the chopped parsley, bring back to a boil, and simmer for 5 minutes. Adjust the seasoning.

6 Serve the soup in warmed bowls with chunks of fresh crusty bread, or put a toasted slice of crusty bread in the base of each bowl before adding the soup. If possible, remove a few half shells from the mussels before serving.

STEP 1

STEP 2

STEP 4

STEP 5

RED BEAN SOUP

Beans feature widely in Italian soups, making them hearty and tasty. If you prefer you can use other varieties of beans in this soup, which is from Tuscany and Lazio.

SERVES 4–6

*scant 1 cup dried red kidney beans, soaked
   overnight
7¹/₂ cups water
1 large ham bone or bacon knuckle
2 carrots, chopped
1 large onion, chopped
2 celery stalks, sliced thinly
1 leek, trimmed, washed, and sliced
1–2 bay leaves
2 tbsp olive oil
2–3 tomatoes, peeled and chopped
1 garlic clove, crushed
1 tbsp tomato paste
4 tbsp arborio or other short-grain rice
1¹/₄–1¹/₂ cups finelyshredded green cabbage
salt and pepper*

1 Drain the beans and put into a saucepan with enough water to cover. Bring to a boil and boil hard for 15 minutes, then reduce the heat and simmer for 45 minutes. (The boiling is essential with kidney beans to kill naturally occurring toxins.) Drain.

2 Put the beans into a clean saucepan with the measured amount of water, ham bone or knuckle, carrots, onion, celery, leek, bay leaves, and olive oil. Bring to a boil, cover, and simmer for 1 hour or until the beans are very tender.

3 Discard the bay leaves and bone, reserving any ham pieces from the bone. Remove a small cupful of the beans and reserve. Liquidize the soup in a food processor or blender and return it to a clean pan.

4 Add the tomatoes, garlic, tomato paste, rice, and plenty of seasoning. Bring back to a boil and simmer for about 15 minutes or until the rice is tender.

5 Add the cabbage and reserved beans and ham and continue to simmer for 5 minutes. Adjust the seasoning and serve very hot. If liked, a piece of toasted crusty bread may be put in the base of each soup bowl before ladling in the soup. If the soup is too thick, add a little boiling water or stock.

MINESTRONE WITH PESTO

One of the many versions of minestrone, which is always full of a variety of vegetables, pasta, and rice, and often includes beans. This soup is flavored with pesto sauce, so often added to pasta dishes.

STEP 1

SERVES 6

scant 1 cup dried cannellini beans, soaked
   overnight
10 cups water or stock
1 large onion, chopped
1 leek, trimmed, washed, and sliced thinly
2 celery stalks, sliced very thinly
2 carrots, chopped
3 tbsp olive oil
2 tomatoes, peeled and chopped roughly
1 zucchini, trimmed and sliced thinly
2 potatoes, peeled and diced
1 cup elbow macaroni (or other small
   macaroni)
salt and pepper
4–6 tbsp grated Parmesan

PESTO:
2 tbsp pine nuts
5 tbsp olive oil
2 bunches fresh basil, stems removed
4–6 garlic cloves, crushed
¾ cup grated Pecorino or Parmesan cheese
salt and pepper

1 Drain the beans, rinse, and place in a saucepan with the measured water or stock. Bring to a boil, cover, and simmer gently for 1 hour.

2 Add the onion, leek, celery, carrots, and oil. Cover and simmer for 4–5 minutes.

3 Add the tomatoes, zucchini, potatoes, macaroni, and seasoning. Cover again and continue to simmer for about 30 minutes or until the beans are very tender.

4 Meanwhile, make the pesto. Fry the pine nuts in 1 tablespoon of the oil until pale brown, then drain. Put the basil into a food processor or blender with the pine nuts and garlic. Process until finely chopped. Gradually add the oil until smooth. Turn into a bowl, add the cheese and seasoning, and mix thoroughly.

5 Stir 1½ tablespoons of the pesto into the soup until well blended, simmer for a further 5 minutes and adjust the seasoning. Serve very hot, sprinkled with the cheese.

PESTO

Store in an airtight container for up to a week in the refrigerator; or freeze (without adding the cheese) for several months.

STEP 2

STEP 3

STEP 5

MOZZARELLA IN CAROZZA

A delicious way of serving cheese, a specialty of Campania and the Abruzzi. The cheese stretches out into melted strings as you cut it to eat. Some versions have prosciutto added, too.

STEP 1

SERVES 4

7 oz Mozzarella cheese
4 slices prosciutto, about 3 oz
8 slices white bread, preferably 2 days old, crusts removed
a little butter for spreading
2–3 eggs
3 tbsp milk
vegetable oil for deep-frying
salt and pepper
flat-leaf parsley, to garnish (optional)

TOMATO AND BELL PEPPER SAUCE:
1 onion, chopped
2 garlic cloves, crushed
3 tbsp olive oil
1 red bell pepper, cored, deseeded, and chopped
15-oz can peeled tomatoes
2 tbsp tomato paste
3 tbsp water
1 tbsp lemon juice

1 First make the sauce: fry the onion and garlic in the oil until soft. Add the bell pepper and continue to cook for a few minutes. Add the tomatoes, tomato paste, water, lemon juice, and seasoning. Bring up to a boil, cover, and simmer for 10–15 minutes or until tender. Cool the sauce a little, then liquidize until smooth and return to a clean pan.

2 Cut the Mozzarella into 4 slices so they are as large as possible; if the cheese is square, cut it into 8 slices. Trim the ham slices to the same size as the cheese.

3 Lightly butter the bread and use the cheese and ham to make 4 sandwiches, pressing the edges well together. If liked, they may be cut in half at this stage. Chill.

4 Lightly beat the eggs with the milk and seasoning in a shallow dish.

5 Carefully dip the sandwiches in the egg mixture until well coated all over, and if possible leave to soak for a few minutes.

6 Heat the oil in a large pan until it just begins to smoke, or until a cube of bread browns in about 30 seconds. Fry the sandwiches in batches until golden brown on both sides. Drain on paper towels and keep warm. Serve the sandwiches hot, with the reheated sauce, and garnished with parsley.

STEP 3

STEP 5

STEP 6

STEP 1

STEP 2

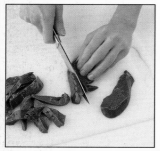

STEP 3

STEP 6

CROSTINI ALLA FIORENTINA

A coarse pâté from Tuscany which can be served as a casual first course or simply spread on small pieces of crusty fried bread (crostini) to serve as an appetizer with drinks.

SERVES 4

3 tbsp olive oil
1 onion, chopped
1 celery stalk, chopped
1 carrot, chopped
1–2 garlic cloves, crushed
³/₄ cup chicken livers
4 oz calf's, lamb's, or pig's liver
²/₃ cup red wine
1 tbsp tomato paste
2 tbsp chopped fresh flat-leaf parsley
3–4 canned anchovy fillets, chopped finely
2 tbsp stock or water
2–3 tbsp butter
1 tbsp capers
salt and pepper
crostini (see right)
chopped fresh parsley, to garnish

1 Heat the oil in a saucepan, add the onion, celery, carrot, and garlic, and cook slowly for 4–5 minutes or until the onion is soft but not colored.

2 Meanwhile, rinse and dry the chicken livers. Dry the calf's or other liver, and slice into strips. Add the liver to the saucepan and fry slowly for a few minutes until the strips are well sealed on all sides.

3 Add half the wine and cook until mostly evaporated, then add the rest of the wine, tomato paste, half the parsley, anchovy fillets, stock or water, a little salt, and plenty of black pepper.

4 Cover the pan and simmer for 15–20 minutes or until tender and most of the liquid has been absorbed.

5 Cool the mixture a little then either coarsely chop or put into a food processor and process until coarsely blended.

6 Return to the pan and add the butter, remaining parsley, and capers and heat through slowly until the butter melts. Adjust the seasoning and turn into a bowl. Serve warm or cold spread on the slices of crusty bread and sprinkled with chopped parsley.

CROSTINI

To make crostini, slice a crusty loaf or a French loaf into small rounds or squares. Heat olive oil in a skillet and fry the slices until golden brown and crisp. Drain on paper towels.

SEAFOOD SALAD

Fresh seafood is plentiful in Italy and varieties of seafood salads are found all over the regions. Each has its own specialty, depending on availability and what appears in each day's catch.

SERVES 4

6 oz squid rings, defrosted if frozen
2½ cups water
⅔ cup dry white wine
8 oz hake or monkfish, cut into cubes
16–20 fresh mussels, scrubbed and beards removed
20 clams in shells, scrubbed, if available (otherwise use extra mussels)
⅓–1 cup peeled shrimp
3–4 scallions, trimmed and sliced (optional)
radicchio and endive leaves, to serve
lemon wedges, to garnish

DRESSING:
6 tbsp olive oil
1 tbsp wine vinegar
2 tbsp chopped fresh parsley
1–2 garlic cloves, crushed
salt and pepper

GARLIC MAYONNAISE:
5 tbsp thick mayonnaise
2–3 tbsp fromage frais or natural yogurt
2 garlic cloves, crushed
1 tbsp capers
2 tbsp chopped fresh parsley or mixed herbs

1 Poach the squid in the water and wine for 20 minutes or until nearly tender. Add the fish cubes and continue to cook slowly for 7–8 minutes or until tender. Strain, reserving the fish, and place the stock in a clean saucepan.

2 Bring the fish stock to a boil and add the mussels and clams. Cover the saucepan and simmer slowly for about 5 minutes or until the shells open. Discard any that stay closed.

3 Drain the shellfish and remove from their shells. Put into a bowl with the cooked fish and add the shrimp and scallions if using.

4 For the dressing, beat together the oil, vinegar, parsley, garlic, salt, and plenty of black pepper. Pour over the fish, mix well, cover, and chill for several hours. Combine all the ingredients for the garlic mayonnaise and chill.

5 Arrange small leaves of radicchio and endive on 4 plates and spoon the fish salad into the center. Garnish each plate with lemon wedges. Serve the garlic mayonnaise with the seafood salad.

CHAPTER TWO

Pasta & Pizza

It is well known that Italians are prolific eaters of pasta, but not everyone realizes just how many varieties of pasta are available; in fact there are many hundreds, and it would be almost impossible to list them all. Home-made pasta only takes a few minutes to cook while the bought variety takes longer, and it is best to follow the cooking directions on the pack. If you are going to make a lot of pasta it is worth investing in a pasta-making machine. Pasta is of Genoese origin but nowadays is even more popular in Naples and the southern regions of Italy, while in the north a fair amount of rice is consumed. Milanese and other risottos are made with short-grain Italian rice, the best of which is Arborio, but remember that this type of rice should never be rinsed before cooking. An Italian risotto is far moister than a pilau or other savoury rice, but it should not be soggy or sticky.

Gnocchi are made from cornmeal, potatoes, or semolina, often combined with spinach and some sort of cheese. They resemble dumplings, and are either poached or baked, and served with some variety of cheese sauce. Polenta is made with either cornmeal or polenta flour and can be served either as a soft porridge or hard cake which is then fried. The traditional method of making polenta involved long, slow cooking, but now there is an excellent polenta mix available which cuts the time to 5 minutes!

Opposite: *The market in the Piazza della Fratta, Padua, offers a wide selection of fruit and vegetables. Italians like to shop daily, to make sure their produce is absolutely fresh.*

STEP 2

STEP 3

STEP 3

STEP 4

TORTELLINI

According to legend the shape of the tortellini is said to resemble the tummy button of Venus. Suffice to say that from this description, when you make tortellini you know exactly what they should look like!

SERVES 4

FILLING:
4 oz boned, skinned chicken breast
2 oz prosciutto
1½ oz cooked spinach, well drained
1 tbsp finely chopped onion
2 tbsp grated Parmesan cheese
good pinch ground allspice
1 egg, beaten
salt and pepper
1 quantity Pasta Dough (see pages 198–9)

SAUCE:
1¼ cups light cream
1–2 garlic cloves, crushed
2 cups thinly sliced button mushrooms
4 tbsp grated Parmesan cheese
1–2 tbsp chopped fresh flat-leaf parsley

1 Poach the chicken in seasoned water until tender, about 10 minutes; drain and chop roughly. When cool, put into a food processor with the prosciutto, spinach, and onion, and process until finely chopped, then add the Parmesan, allspice, egg, and seasoning.

2 Roll out the pasta dough, half at a time, on a lightly floured counter until thin.

3 Cut the dough into 1½–2 in. rounds using a plain cutter. Place ½ teaspoon of the filling in the center of each dough circle, fold the pieces in half to make a semi-circle, and press the edges firmly together. Wrap around your index finger and cross over the 2 ends, pressing firmly together, curling the rest of the dough backwards to make a "tummy button" shape. Slip the tortellini off your finger and lay it on a lightly floured tray. Repeat with the rest of the dough, rerolling the trimmings.

4 Cook the tortellini in batches: heat a large pan of salted boiling water and add some tortellini. Bring back to a boil and once they rise to the surface cook for about 5 minutes, stirring occasionally. Remove with a perforated spoon, drain on paper towels and keep warm in a serving dish while cooking the remainder.

5 To make the sauce, heat the cream with the garlic in a pan and bring to a boil; simmer for a few minutes. Add the mushrooms and half the Parmesan, season, and simmer for 2–3 minutes. Stir in the parsley and pour over the warm tortellini. Sprinkle the tortellini with the remaining Parmesan and serve.

SICILIAN SPAGHETTI

*This delicious Sicilian dish originated as a handy way of using up
leftover cooked pasta. Any variety of long pasta could be used.*

STEP 1

SERVES 4
OVEN: 400°F

2 eggplants, about 1¼ lb in total
⅔ cup olive oil
12 oz lean beef, finely ground
1 onion, chopped
2 garlic cloves, crushed
2 tbsp tomato paste
15-oz can peeled tomatoes, chopped
1 tsp Worcestershire sauce
1 tsp freshly chopped oregano or marjoram
   or ½ tsp dried oregano or marjoram
¼ cup sliced pitted black olives
1 green, red, or yellow bell pepper, cored,
   deseeded, and chopped
6 oz spaghetti
1 cup grated Parmesan cheese
salt and pepper
oregano or parsley, to garnish (optional)

1 Brush an 8-in. springform pan with
olive oil, place a disc of baking
parchment in the base, and oil. Trim the
eggplants and cut into slanting slices
about ¼ in. thick. Heat some of the oil in a
skillet. Fry a few slices at a time in hot oil
until lightly browned, turning once, and
adding more oil as necessary. Drain on
paper towels.

2 Put the ground beef, onion, and
garlic into a saucepan and cook,
stirring frequently, until browned all
over. Add the tomato paste, tomatoes,
Worcestershire sauce, herbs, and
seasoning and simmer for 10 minutes,
stirring occasionally, then add the olives
and bell pepper, and continue for a
further 10 minutes.

STEP 3

3 Heat a large pan of salted water
and cook the spaghetti for 12–14
minutes until tender. Drain thoroughly.
Turn the spaghetti into a bowl and mix
in the meat mixture and Parmesan,
combining thoroughly using 2 forks.

4 Lay overlapping slices of eggplant
evenly over the base of the springform pan and up the sides. Add the meat
mixture, pressing it down, and cover
with the remaining slices of eggplant.

STEP 4

5 Stand in a roasting pan and cook in
a preheated oven for 40 minutes.
Let stand for 5 minutes. Loosen around
the edges and invert on to a warmed
serving dish, releasing the pan's clip.
Remove the parchment. Sprinkle with
herbs before serving, if liked. Extra
Parmesan may be offered.

STEP 4

GNOCCHI ROMANA

*This is a traditional recipe from Piedmont. For a less rich version, omit
the eggs. This is often served before a light main course, but it also
makes an excellent main meal with a crisp salad.*

STEP 1

STEP 2

SERVES 4
OVEN: 400°F

3 cups milk
¼ tsp grated nutmeg
6 tbsp butter, plus extra for greasing
1⅓ cups semolina
1 cup finely grated Parmesan cheese
2 eggs, beaten
½ cup grated Gruyère cheese
salt and pepper
basil sprigs, to garnish

1 Bring the milk to a boil, remove
from the heat and stir in the
nutmeg, 2 tablespoons butter, and the
seasonings. Whisk in the semolina
gradually to prevent lumps forming and
return to a low heat. Simmer slowly for
about 10 minutes, stirring constantly,
until very thick.

2 Beat ½ cup Parmesan into the
semolina, followed by the eggs.
Continue beating until the mixture is
quite smooth.

3 Spread out the semolina mixture in
an even layer on a sheet of baking
parchment or in a large oiled roasting
pan, smoothing the surface with a wet
spatula – it should be about ½ in. thick.

Leave until cold, then chill for about
1 hour until firm.

4 Cut the gnocchi into circles of
about 1½ in., using a plain greased
cookie cutter.

5 Thoroughly grease a shallow
ovenproof dish, or 4 individual
dishes. Lay the gnocchi trimmings in the
base of the dish and cover with
overlapping circles of gnocchi. Melt the
remaining butter and drizzle all over the
gnocchi, then sprinkle first with the
remaining Parmesan, and then with the
grated Gruyère.

6 Cook in a preheated oven for
25–30 minutes until the top is
crisp and golden brown.

STEP 3

STEP 4

NOTE

Tomato and Bell Pepper Sauce (see page
21) may be served with this dish, if liked.

POLENTA

Polenta is prepared and served in a variety of ways and can be enjoyed hot or cold, sweet or savoury. This is the traditional way of making it in Lombardy, although there is now an instant polenta mix available.

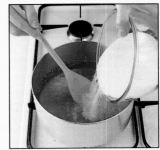
STEP 1

SERVES 4

7 cups water
1¹/₂ tsp salt
2 cups polenta or cornmeal flour
vegetable oil for frying and oiling
2 eggs, beaten (optional)
2 cups fresh fine white bread crumbs
    (optional)

MUSHROOM SAUCE:
3 tbsp olive oil
4 cups sliced mushrooms
2 garlic cloves, crushed
²/₃ cup dry white wine
4 tbsp heavy cream
2 tbsp chopped mixed fresh herbs
salt and pepper

1 Bring the water and salt to a boil in a large saucepan and gradually sprinkle in the polenta or cornmeal flour, stirring constantly, to make sure the mixture is smooth, without lumps.

2 Simmer the mixture slowly, stirring frequently, until the polenta is thick, 30–35 minutes. It may splatter so partially cover the saucepan with a lid. The mixture should be thick enough for a wooden spoon to almost stand upright in it on its own.

3 Thoroughly oil a shallow pan, about 11 × 7 in., and spoon in the polenta. Spread out evenly, using a wet spatula, if necessary. Leave until cold, then leave for a few hours at room temperature, if possible.

4 Cut the polenta into 30–36 squares. Heat the oil in a skillet and fry for about 5 minutes until the pieces are golden brown all over, turning them several times. Alternatively, dip each piece of polenta in beaten egg and coat in bread crumbs before frying in the hot oil.

5 To make the mushroom sauce: heat the oil in a pan and fry the mushrooms with the crushed garlic for 3–4 minutes. Add the wine, season well, and simmer for 5 minutes. Add the cream and chopped herbs and simmer for another minute or so.

6 Serve the polenta with the mushroom sauce. It could also be served with a tomato sauce, if preferred.

STEP 2

STEP 3

STEP 4

STEP 1

STEP 2

STEP 4

STEP 5

MILANESE RISOTTO

Italian rice is a round, short-grained variety with a nutty flavor, which is essential for a good risotto. Arborio is the very best kind to use.

SERVES 4–5

2 good pinches saffron threads
1 large onion, chopped finely
1–2 garlic cloves, crushed
6 tbsp butter
1²/₃ cups Arborio or other short-grain
  Italian rice
²/₃ cup dry white wine
5 cups boiling beef, chicken, or vegetable
  stock
³/₄ cup grated Parmesan cheese
salt and pepper

1 Put the saffron in a small bowl, cover with 3–4 tablespoons boiling water and let soak while cooking the risotto.

2 Fry the onion and garlic in 4 tablespoons of the butter until soft but not colored. Add the rice and continue to cook for a few minutes until all the grains are coated in butter and beginning to color lightly.

3 Add the wine to the rice and simmer slowly, stirring from time to time until it is all absorbed.

4 Add the boiling stock a little at a time, about ²/₃ cup, cooking until

the liquid is fully absorbed before adding more, and stirring frequently.

5 When all the stock is absorbed the rice should be tender but not soft and soggy. Stir in the saffron liquid, Parmesan, remaining butter, and plenty of seasoning and simmer for a minute or so until piping hot and thoroughly mixed together.

6 Cover the pan tightly and leave to stand for 5 minutes off the heat. Give a good stir and serve at once.

COOKING RISOTTO

The finished dish should have moist but separate grains. This is achieved by adding the hot stock a little at a time, only adding more when the last addition is fully absorbed. Don't leave the risotto to cook by itself: it needs constant watching to see when more liquid is required.

STEP 1

STEP 2

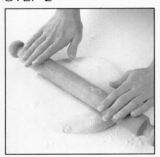

STEP 3

STEP 3

CALABRIAN PIZZA

Traditionally, a Calabrian pizza has a double layer of dough to make it robust and filling, but it can also be made as a single-layer pizza as shown here. Just double the amount of filling to make two single-layer pizzas.

SERVES 4–6
OVEN: 350°F

3½ cups all-purpose flour
½ tsp salt
1 envelope easy-blend yeast
2 tbsp olive oil
about 1 cup plus 2 tbsp warm water

FILLING:
2 tbsp olive oil
2 garlic cloves, crushed
1 red bell pepper, cored, deseeded, and sliced
1 yellow bell pepper, cored, deseeded, and
    sliced
4 oz Ricotta cheese
6 oz sun-dried tomatoes in oil, drained
3 hard-cooked eggs, sliced thinly
1 tbsp chopped mixed fresh herbs
4 oz salami, cut into strips
5–6 oz Mozzarella cheese, grated
a little milk, to glaze
salt and pepper

1 Sift the flour and salt into a bowl and mix in the yeast, then add the oil and enough warm water to mix to a smooth dough. Knead for 10–15 minutes by hand, or for 5 minutes with an electric mixer with a dough hook.

2 Shape the dough into a ball, place in a lightly oiled polythene bag, and put in a warm place for 1–1½ hours or until doubled in size.

3 Heat the oil in a skillet and fry the garlic and bell peppers slowly in the oil until soft. Punch down the dough and roll out half to fit the base of a 12 × 10-in. oiled roasting pan. Season and spread with the Ricotta, then cover with the tomatoes, eggs, herbs, and pepper mixture. Arrange the salami strips on top and sprinkle with the grated cheese.

4 Roll out the remaining dough and place over the filling, pressing the edges together, or use to make a second pizza. Put to rise for about 1 hour in a warm place until puffed up. A single-layer pizza will take 30–40 minutes to rise.

5 Prick the double pizza with a fork about 20 times, brush the top with milk and bake for 50 minutes or until browned and firm. The single-layer pizza will take only 35–40 minutes. Serve hot.

CHAPTER THREE

Fish & Shellfish

Italians eat everything that comes out of the sea, from the smallest whitebait to the massive tuna fish, not forgetting the wide variety of shellfish. Fish markets in Italy are fascinating, with a huge variety of fish on display, but as most of the fish comes from the Mediterranean it is not always easy to find an equivalent elsewhere. However, imported frozen fish of all kinds is now appearing in fish shops and supermarkets.

After pasta, fish is probably the most important source of food in Italy, and in many recipes fish or shellfish is combined with one type of pasta or another. The inland regions of Italy such as Lombardy and Umbria have lakes with plentiful supplies of fish, while Apulia has abundant supplies caught by offshore trawlers. The south has splendid fish, with tuna and swordfish taking pride of place, although red mullet and sea bass are plentiful and popular, too. Venice and surrounding areas have a wealth of fish and shellfish recipes, often combined with pasta, while the Ligurian coast is popular for fish soups and stews. The islands of Sicily and Sardinia abound with fish, which feature widely in their cuisine, from the large tuna to the sardines that give Sardinia its name.

Opposite: *The fishing fleet prepares to set off in the early morning light. Later in the day the catch – anything from John Dory, sea bass, mullet, snapper, and squid to lobsters and crabs – will be proudly displayed on the quayside, ready for the seafood market.*

STEP 2

STEP 2

STEP 4

STEP 4

BAKED SEA BASS

Sea bass is a delicious white-fleshed fish with a wonderful fresh flavor. If cooking two small fish, they can be broiled; if cooking one large fish, bake it in the oven.

SERVES 4
OVEN: 375°F

3 lb sea bass or 2 × 1½ lb sea bass, gutted
2–4 sprigs fresh rosemary
½ lemon, sliced thinly
2 tbsp olive oil
bay leaves and lemon wedges, to garnish

GARLIC SAUCE:
2 tsp coarse sea salt
2 tsp capers
2 garlic cloves, crushed
4 tbsp water
2 fresh bay leaves
1 tsp lemon juice or wine vinegar
2 tbsp olive oil
black pepper

1 Scrape off the scales from the fish and cut off the sharp fins. Make diagonal cuts along both sides. Wash and dry thoroughly.

2 Place a sprig of rosemary in the cavity of each of the smaller fish with half the lemon slices; or 2 sprigs and all the lemon in the large fish. To broil, place in a foil-lined pan, brush lightly with 1–2 tablespoons oil, and broil under a medium heat for about 5 minutes on each side or until cooked through, turning carefully.

3 To bake, place the fish in a foil-lined dish or roasting pan brushed with oil, and brush the fish with the rest of the oil. Bake in a preheated oven for about 30 minutes for the small fish or 45–50 minutes for the large fish, until tender when tested with a skewer.

4 To make the sauce: crush the salt and capers with the garlic in a mortar and pestle if available and then gradually work in the water. Alternatively, put it all into a food processor or blender and liquidize until smooth. Bruise the bay leaves and remaining sprigs of rosemary and put in a bowl. Add the garlic mixture, lemon juice or vinegar, and oil and pound together until the flavors are released. Season with black pepper.

5 Place the fish on a serving dish and, if liked, carefully remove the skin. Spoon some of the sauce over the fish and serve the rest separately. Garnish with fresh bay leaves and lemon wedges.

STEP 2

STEP 4

STEP 5

STEP 5

SARDINE & POTATO BAKE

Fresh sardines bear very little resemblance to the canned varieties. They are readily available, frozen and sometimes fresh, so this traditional dish from Liguria can now be enjoyed by all.

SERVES 4
OVEN: 375°F

2 lb potatoes, peeled
2 lb sardines, defrosted if frozen
1 tbsp olive oil, plus extra for oiling
1 onion, chopped
2–3 garlic cloves, crushed
2 tbsp chopped fresh flat-leaf parsley
12 oz ripe tomatoes, peeled and sliced or 1 5-oz can peeled tomatoes, partly drained and chopped
1–2 tbsp chopped fresh Italian herbs (e.g. oregano, thyme, rosemary, marjoram)
$^{2}/_{3}$ cup dry white wine
salt and pepper

1 Put the potatoes in a saucepan of salted water, bring to a boil, cover, and simmer for 10 minutes, then drain. When cool enough to handle, cut into slices about ¼ in. thick.

2 Gut and clean the sardines: cut off their heads and tails and then slit open the length of the belly. Turn the fish over so the skin is upwards and press firmly along the backbone to loosen the bones. Turn over again and carefully remove the backbone. Wash the fish in cold water, drain well, and dry them on paper towels.

3 Heat the oil in a saucepan and fry the onion and garlic until soft, but not colored.

4 Arrange the potatoes in a well-oiled ovenproof dish and sprinkle with the onion and garlic and then the parsley and plenty of seasoning.

5 Lay the open sardines over the potatoes, skin-side down, then cover with the tomatoes and the rest of the herbs. Pour on the wine and season again.

6 Cook uncovered in a preheated oven for about 40 minutes until the fish is tender. If the casserole seems to be drying out, add another 2 tablespoons of wine.

VARIATION

Fresh anchovies may be used in this recipe in place of sardines. Prepare in the same way.

STEP 1

STEP 3

STEP 4

STEP 5

TROUT IN RED WINE

This recipe from Trentino is best when the fish are freshly caught, but it is a good way to cook any trout, giving it an interesting flavor.

SERVES 4

4 fresh trout, about 10 oz each
1 cup red- or white-wine vinegar
1¼ cups red or dry white wine
⅔ cup water
1 carrot, sliced
2–4 bay leaves
thinly pared rind of 1 lemon
1 small onion, sliced very thinly
4 sprigs fresh parsley
4 sprigs fresh thyme
1 tsp black peppercorns
6–8 whole cloves
6 tbsp butter
1 tbsp chopped fresh mixed herbs
  or parsley
salt and pepper
fresh herbs and lemon slices, to garnish

1 Gut the trout but leave their heads on. Dry on paper towels and lay the fish head to tail in a shallow container or roasting pan just large enough to hold them in a single layer.

2 Bring the wine vinegar to a boil and pour slowly all over the fish. Let the fish marinate for about 20 minutes.

3 Put the wine, water, carrot, bay leaves, lemon rind, onion, herbs, peppercorns, and cloves into a saucepan with a good pinch of sea salt and heat slowly.

4 Drain the fish thoroughly, discarding the vinegar. Place the fish in a fish kettle or large skillet so they touch. When the wine mixture boils, strain over the fish so they are about half covered. Cover the pan and simmer very slowly over a low heat for 15 minutes.

5 Carefully remove the fish from the liquid, draining off as much as possible, and arrange on a serving dish.

6 Boil the cooking liquid hard until it is reduced to 4–6 tablespoons. Melt the butter in a small saucepan and strain in the cooking liquid. Adjust the seasoning and spoon the sauce over the fish. Sprinkle with chopped mixed herbs and garnish with lemon and sprigs of fresh herbs.

STEP 1

STEP 1

STEP 2

STEP 3

SQUID CASSEROLE

Squid and octopus are great favorites in Italy and around the Mediterranean resorts. Squid is often served fried, but here it is casseroled with tomatoes and bell peppers to give a rich sauce.

SERVES 4
OVEN: 350°F

2 lb whole squid or 1½ lb squid rings,
    defrosted if frozen
3 tbsp olive oil
1 large onion, sliced thinly
2 garlic cloves, crushed
1 red bell pepper, cored, deseeded, and sliced
1–2 sprigs fresh rosemary
⅔ cup dry white wine and 1 cup water, or
    1½ cups water or fish stock
15-oz can peeled tomatoes, chopped
2 tbsp tomato paste
1 tsp paprika
salt and pepper
fresh rosemary or parsley sprigs, to garnish
    (optional)

1 Prepare the squid (see below right) and cut into ½-in. slices; cut the tentacles into lengths of about 2 in. If using frozen squid rings, make sure they are fully defrosted and well drained.

2 Heat the oil in a flameproof casserole and fry the onion and garlic slowly until soft. Add the squid rings, increase the heat, and continue to cook for about 10 minutes until sealed and beginning to color slightly. Add the red bell pepper, rosemary, and wine (if

using), and water or stock and bring up to a boil. Cover and simmer slowly for 45 minutes.

3 Discard the rosemary sprigs (but don't take out any leaves that have come off). Add the tomatoes, tomato paste, seasoning, and paprika. Continue to simmer slowly for 45–60 minutes, or cover the casserole tightly and cook in a preheated oven for 45–60 minutes until tender.

4 Give the sauce a good stir and adjust the seasoning. Garnish with rosemary or parsley, if liked, and serve with lots of crusty bread.

TO PREPARE SQUID

Peel off as much as possible of the fine outer skin, using your fingers, then cut off the head and tentacles. Extract the transparent flat oval bone from the body and discard. Carefully remove the sac of black ink, then turn the body sac inside out. Wash thoroughly in cold water. Cut off the tentacles from the head and discard the rest; wash thoroughly.

CHAPTER FOUR

Meat & Poultry

Italians tend to have their own special way of butchering meat, producing very different cuts. Most of their meat is sold boned and often cut straight across the grain. They tend to serve prime cuts and steaks very rare, so great care needs to be taken when ordering in a restaurant. Veal is a great favorite in Italy and widely available, with the popular cuts for scallops always made straight across the grain of the meat. It is then beaten out thinly, using a meat mallet. Pork is also popular, with roast pig the traditional dish of Umbria. Suckling pig is roasted with lots of fresh herbs, especially rosemary, until the skin is crisp and brown. Lamb is often served for special occasions, cooked on a spit or roasted in the oven with wine, garlic, and herbs; and the very small cutlets from young lambs feature widely, especially in Rome. Variety meats play an important role in Italian cooking with liver, brains, sweetbreads, tongue, heart, tripe, and kidneys, from both veal and lamb, always available.

Poultry dishes provide some of Italy's finest food. Every part of the chicken is used, including the feet and innards for making soup. It is the spit-roasted chicken, flavored strongly with rosemary, that has become almost a national Italian dish, being sold all over the country. Turkey, duck, goose, and guinea fowl are also popular, as is game. Wild rabbit and hare, wild boar and deer are also available, especially in Sardinia.

Opposite: *Italians take their food very seriously, so eating out is a very popular activity. Blessed with a wonderful climate, they can often eat outdoors, as in this Venetian restaurant.*

PIZZAIOLA STEAK

This has a Neapolitan sauce, using the delicious red tomatoes so abundant in that area, but canned ones make an excellent alternative.

STEP 3

SERVES 4

2 x 15-oz can peeled tomatoes or 1¹/₂ lb
   fresh tomatoes
4 tbsp olive oil
2–3 garlic cloves, crushed
1 onion, chopped finely
1 tbsp tomato paste
1¹/₂ tsp freshly chopped marjoram or
   oregano or ³/₄ tsp dried marjoram or
   oregano
4 thin sirloin or rump steaks
2 tbsp chopped fresh flat-leaf parsley
1 tsp sugar
salt and pepper
fresh herbs, to garnish (optional)
sautéed potatoes, to serve

1 If using canned tomatoes, liquidize them in a food processor, then strain to remove the seeds. If using fresh tomatoes, peel, remove the seeds, and chop finely.

2 Heat half the oil in a saucepan and fry the garlic and onions very slowly for about 5 minutes until soft.

3 Add the tomatoes, seasoning, tomato paste, and chopped herbs to the saucepan. If using fresh tomatoes, add 4 tablespoons water too, and then simmer very slowly for 8–10 minutes, giving an occasional stir.

4 Meanwhile, trim the steaks if necessary and season with salt and pepper. Heat the remaining oil in a skillet and fry the steaks quickly on both sides to seal, then continue until cooked to your liking – 2 minutes for rare, 3–4 minutes for medium, or 5 minutes for well done. Alternatively, cook the steaks under a hot broiler after brushing lightly with oil.

5 When the sauce has thickened a little, adjust the seasoning and stir in the chopped parsley and sugar to taste.

6 Pour off the excess fat from the skillet with the steaks and add the tomato sauce. Reheat slowly and serve at once, with the sauce spooned over and around the steaks. Garnish with fresh herbs, if liked. Sautéed potatoes make a good accompaniment with a green vegetable.

ALTERNATIVE

This sauce can be served with veal and chicken. It can also be served with broiled or baked white fish.

STEP 4

STEP 5

STEP 6

STEP 1

STEP 2

STEP 3

STEP 4

VITELLO TONNATO

Veal dishes are the specialty of Lombardy, with this dish being one of the more sophisticated. Serve cold, either as part of an antipasto or as a main course. It is best served with seasonal salads.

SERVES 4

1½ lb boned leg of veal, rolled
2 bay leaves
10 black peppercorns
2–3 whole cloves
½ tsp salt
2 carrots, sliced
1 onion, sliced
2 celery stalks, sliced
about 3 cups stock or water
⅔ cup dry white wine (optional)

TUNA SAUCE:
3 oz canned tuna fish, well drained
1½ oz-can anchovy fillets, drained
⅔ cup olive oil
2 tsp capers
2 egg yolks
1 tbsp lemon juice
salt and pepper

TO GARNISH:
capers
lemon wedges
fresh herbs

1 Put the veal in a saucepan with the bay leaves, peppercorns, cloves, salt, and vegetables. Add sufficient stock or water and the wine (if using) to barely cover the veal. Bring to a boil, remove any foam, then cover the saucepan and simmer slowly for 1 hour or until tender. Leave in the water until cold, then drain thoroughly. If time allows, chill the veal once it is cool to make it easier to carve.

2 To make the tuna sauce: mash the tuna fish with 4 anchovy fillets and 1 tablespoon oil and the capers, then add the egg yolks and press the mixture through a strainer or liquidize in a food processor or blender until smooth.

3 Stir in the lemon juice then gradually beat in the rest of the oil a few drops at a time until the sauce is smooth and has the consistency of thick cream. Season to taste.

4 Slice the veal thinly and arrange on a flat platter in overlapping slices. Spoon the tuna fish sauce over the veal to cover. Then cover the dish and chill overnight.

5 Before serving, uncover the veal and arrange the remaining anchovy fillets and the capers in a decorative pattern on top. Garnish with lemon wedges and herbs.

STEP 1

STEP 3

STEP 4

STEP 6

POT ROAST LEG OF LAMB

This dish from the Abruzzi is even better if you use a leg of mutton in place of lamb: the meat absorbs the flavors even better and becomes very tender, giving a truly memorable dish.

SERVES 4
OVEN: 350°F

3½ lb leg of lamb
3–4 sprigs fresh rosemary
4 oz bacon slices
4 tbsp olive oil
2–3 garlic cloves, crushed
2 onions, sliced
2 carrots, sliced
2 celery stalks, sliced
1¼ cups dry white wine
1 tbsp tomato paste
1¼ cups stock
12 oz tomatoes, peeled, quartered, and
    seeded
1 tbsp chopped fresh flat-leaf parsley
1 tbsp chopped fresh oregano or marjoram
salt and pepper
fresh rosemary sprigs, to garnish

1 Wipe the lamb all over, trim off any excess fat, then season well with salt and pepper, rubbing well in. Lay the fresh rosemary sprigs over the lamb, cover evenly with the bacon slices and tie in place with fine kitchen string.

2 Heat the oil in a skillet and fry the lamb for about 10 minutes until browned all over, turning it over several times. Remove the lamb from the skillet.

3 Transfer the oil from the skillet to a large flameproof casserole and fry the garlic and onions together for 3–4 minutes until beginning to soften. Add the carrots and celery and continue to cook for a few minutes longer, stirring occasionally.

4 Lay the lamb on top of the vegetables and press well to partly bury. Pour the wine over the lamb, add the tomato paste and simmer for 3–4 minutes. Add the stock, tomatoes, herbs, and plenty of seasoning and bring back to a boil for a further 3–4 minutes.

5 Cover the casserole tightly and cook in a preheated oven for 2–2½ hours until very tender.

6 Remove the lamb from the casserole and if liked, take off the bacon and herbs along with the string. Keep warm. Strain the juices, skimming off any excess fat, and serve in a pitcher. The vegetables may be put around the lamb or in a serving dish. Garnish with fresh rosemary sprigs.

SALTIMBOCCA

Literally translated saltimbocca means "jump in the mouth", and this quick, tasty veal dish almost does that.

STEP 2

STEP 3

STEP 4

STEP 5

SERVES 4

4 thin veal scallops
8 fresh sage leaves
4 thin slices prosciutto, same size as the veal
flour for dredging
2 tbsp olive oil
2 tbsp butter
4 tbsp white wine
4 tbsp chicken stock
4 tbsp Marsala
salt and pepper
fresh sage leaves, to garnish

1 Either leave the scallops as they are or cut in half. Place the pieces of veal on a sheet of plastic wrap or baking parchment, keeping them well apart, and cover with a second sheet.

2 Using a meat mallet or rolling pin, beat the scallops slowly until they are at least twice their original size and very thin.

3 Lightly season the scallops with salt and pepper and lay 2 fresh sage leaves on the large slices, or one on each of the smaller slices. Then lay the prosciutto evenly over the scallops to cover the sage and fit the size of the veal.

4 Secure the prosciutto to the veal with wooden toothpicks. If preferred, the large slices can be folded in half first. Dredge lightly with flour.

5 Heat the olive oil and butter in a large skillet and fry the scallops until golden brown each side and just cooked through – about 4 minutes for single slices or 5–6 minutes for double ones. Take care not to overcook. Remove to a serving dish and keep warm.

6 Add the wine, stock, and Marsala to the pan and bring to a boil, stirring to loosen all the sediment from the pan. Boil until reduced by almost half. Adjust the seasoning and quickly pour over the saltimbocca. Serve at once, garnished with fresh sage leaves.

ALTERNATIVE

This dish can also be made using boned chicken breast halves. Slit the pieces almost in half, open out, and beat as thinly as possible, as for the veal.

CHICKEN WITH GREEN OLIVES

Olives are a popular flavoring for poultry and game in Apulia, where this recipe originates. In Italy every morsel of the bird is used in some way, most often for soups and stock.

STEP 1

SERVES 4
OVEN: 350°F

4 chicken breast halves, part boned
2 tbsp olive oil
2 tbsp butter
1 large onion, chopped finely
2 garlic cloves, crushed
2 red, yellow, or green bell peppers, cored, deseeded, and cut into large pieces
8 oz large closed-cup mushrooms, sliced or quartered
6 oz tomatoes, peeled and halved
²/₃ cup dry white wine
4–6 oz green olives, pitted
4–6 tbsp heavy cream
salt and pepper
chopped fresh flat-leaf parsley, to garnish

STEP 2

1 Season the chicken. Heat the oil and butter in a skillet. Add the chicken and fry until browned all over. Remove from the skillet.

2 Add the onion and garlic and fry slowly until beginning to soften. Add the bell peppers with the mushrooms and continue to cook for a few minutes longer.

3 Add the tomatoes and plenty of seasoning and then transfer the vegetable mixture to an ovenproof casserole. Place the chicken on the bed of vegetables.

STEP 3

4 Add the wine to the skillet and bring to a boil. Pour the wine over the chicken and cover the casserole tightly. Cook in a preheated oven for 50 minutes.

5 Add the olives to the chicken, mix lightly then pour on the cream. Re-cover the casserole and return to the oven for 10–20 minutes or until the chicken is very tender.

6 Adjust the seasoning and serve the pieces of chicken, surrounded by the vegetables and sauce, with pasta or tiny new potatoes. Sprinkle with parsley to garnish.

NOODLES

Serve this dish with freshly made ribbon noodles for a really attractive presentation. Fresh pasta takes only 2–3 minutes to cook.

STEP 5

CHAPTER FIVE

Desserts

Many Italians prefer to finish their meal with a bowl of mixed fruits or fruits with cheese, but they do like their desserts too. When there is a family gathering or a celebration, a special effort is made and the delicacies appear. The Sicilians are said to have the sweetest tooth of all, and many Italian desserts are thought to have originated there. Ice cream (*gelato*), sorbet, and water ice (*granita*) are said to be borrowed from the Arabs, who occupied Sicily centuries ago, and you have to go a very long way to beat a Sicilian ice cream, especially the famous cassata and Ricotta ice creams.

Fruits feature in desserts too. The famous pear tarts of the north are mouthwatering, using the very best fruit blended with apricot jam, golden raisins and almonds, while oranges appear marinated in syrup and liqueur. Cookies with almond flavoring are often served as an accompaniment, and the famous florentines – cookies full of candied fruit and covered with chocolate – are favorites. Cakes are also popular, often incorporating Mascarpone or Ricotta along with citrus fruits and honey. Tiramisu is a favorite with all, and for Christmas and special occasions try the honey cake from Siena called Panforte – so very rich that even a tiny piece will leave you with delicious memories for a very long time.

Opposite: *The fertile plains of Tuscany grow an enormous variety of fruit and vegetables. Many famous desserts originate here, including the luscious Panforte di Siena.*

STEP 1

STEP 1

STEP 4

STEP 5

TIRAMISU

A favorite Italian dessert which is found in many regions. Here it is flavored with coffee and Amaretto, but you could also use Marsala and Maraschino.

SERVES 4–6

20–24 ladyfingers, about 5 oz
2 tbsp cold black coffee
2 tbsp coffee extract
2 tbsp Amaretto or brandy
4 egg yolks
6 tbsp superfine sugar
few drops vanilla extract
grated rind of ½ lemon
1½ cups Mascarpone cheese
2 tsp lemon juice
1 cup heavy cream
1 tbsp milk
¼ cup slivered almonds, lightly toasted
2 tbsp cocoa powder
1 tbsp confectioners' sugar

1 Arrange almost half the ladyfingers in the base of a glass bowl or serving dish. Combine the black coffee, coffee extract, and Amaretto or brandy and sprinkle just over half the mixture over the fingers.

2 Put the egg yolks into a heatproof bowl with the sugar, vanilla extract, and lemon rind. Stand over a saucepan of slowly simmering water and beat until very thick and creamy and the whisk leaves a very heavy trail when lifted from the bowl.

3 Put the Mascarpone into a bowl, add the lemon juice, and beat until the mixture is smooth.

4 Combine the egg mixture and Mascarpone mixture until evenly blended, then pour half over the ladyfingers and spread out evenly.

5 Add another layer of ladyfingers, sprinkle with the remaining coffee mixture, and then cover with the remaining cheese mixture. Chill for at least 2 hours and preferably overnight.

6 To serve, whip the cream and milk together until fairly stiff and spread or pipe over the dessert. Sprinkle with the slivered almonds and then sift an even layer of cocoa powder over so the top is completely covered. Finally sift a very light layer of confectioners' sugar over the cocoa powder.

ZABAGLIONE

This light dessert is reminiscent of a whipped egg custard. Serve warm or chilled, accompanied by ladyfingers or amaretti cookies, and soft fruits such as strawberries or raspberries.

STEP 1

SERVES 4

6 egg yolks
6 tbsp superfine sugar
6 tbsp Marsala
amaretti cookies or ladyfingers (optional)
strawberries or raspberries (optional)

1 Put the egg yolks into a heatproof bowl and beat until a pale yellow color, using a rotary, balloon, or electric whisk.

2 Beat in the sugar, followed by the Marsala, continuing to beat all the time.

3 Stand the bowl over a saucepan of very slowly simmering water, or transfer to the top of a double boiler, and continue to beat constantly, scraping around the sides of the bowl from time to time. Beat until the mixture thickens sufficiently to stand in soft peaks. On no account allow the water to boil or the zabaglione will overcook and turn into scrambled eggs.

4 As soon as the mixture is thick and foamy, take it from the heat and beat for a couple of minutes longer.

5 Pour immediately into stemmed glasses and serve warm, or leave until cold and serve chilled.

6 Fruits such as strawberries or raspberries or crumbled ladyfingers or amaretti cookies may be placed in the base of the glasses before adding the zabaglione.

STEP 2

STEP 3

> ### VARIATION
>
> Any other type of liqueur may be used in place of Marsala, for a change.

STEP 4

STEP 1

STEP 2

STEP 3

STEP 4

PANFORTE DI SIENA

This famous Tuscan honey and nut cake is a Christmas specialty. In Italy it is sold in pretty boxes, which seems to make it taste even better. Panforte is very rich and sticky and should be served in very thin slices.

SERVES 12
OVEN: 300°F

1 cup split whole almonds
³/₄ cup hazelnuts
¹/₂ cup cut candied peel
¹/₂ cup no-need-to-soak dried apricots
¹/₂ cup candied or crystallized pineapple
grated rind of 1 large orange
¹/₂ cup all-purpose flour
2 tbsp cocoa powder
2 tsp ground cinnamon
¹/₂ cup superfine sugar
¹/₂ cup honey
confectioners' sugar for dredging

1 Toast the almonds until lightly browned and place in a bowl. Toast the hazelnuts under the broiler until the skins split. Place the hazelnuts on a towel and rub off the skins with the towel. Roughly chop the hazelnuts and add to the almonds with the candied peel.

2 Chop the apricots and pineapple fairly finely, add to the nuts with the orange rind, and mix well.

3 Sift the flour with the cocoa and cinnamon, add to the nut mixture, and mix evenly.

4 Line a round 8-in. cake pan or deep loose-bottom pie pan with baking parchment.

5 Put the sugar and honey into a saucepan and heat until the sugar dissolves, then boil slowly for about 5 minutes or until the mixture thickens and begins to turn a deeper shade of brown. Quickly add to the nut mixture and stir through it evenly. Turn into the prepared pan and level the top with the help of a damp spoon.

6 Bake in a preheated oven for 1 hour. Remove from the oven and leave in the pan until cold. Take out of the pan and carefully peel off the parchment. Dredge the cake heavily with sifted confectioners' sugar. Serve cut into very thin slices.

STORAGE

Panforte will keep for several weeks stored in an airtight container or securely wrapped in foil.

PEAR TART

Pears are a very popular fruit in Italy. In this recipe from Trentino they are flavored with almonds, cinnamon, raisins, and apricot jam, then baked in an open tart with a soft-textured sweet pastry shell.

STEP 1

Serves 4–6
Oven: 400°F

2¼ cups all-purpose flour
pinch salt
½ cup superfine sugar
½ cup butter, diced
1 egg
1 egg yolk
few drops vanilla extract
2–3 tsp water

FILLING:
4 tbsp apricot jam
2 oz amaretti or ratafia cookies, crumbled
1¾–2 lb pears, peeled and cored
1 tsp ground cinnamon
½ cup raisins or golden raisins
⅓ cup soft brown sugar
sifted confectioners' sugar for dredging

1 Sift the flour and salt on to a flat surface, make a well in the center, and add the sugar, butter, egg, egg yolk, vanilla, and most of the water.

2 Using your fingers, gradually work the flour into the other ingredients to give a smooth pliable dough, adding a little more water, if necessary. Wrap in plastic wrap and chill for 1 hour or until firm. Alternatively, put all the ingredients into a food processor and process until evenly blended and smooth.

3 Roll out almost three-quarters of the dough and line a shallow 10-in. pie pan. Spread the apricot jam over the base and sprinkle with the crushed cookies.

4 Slice the pears very thinly. Arrange the pear slices over the cookies in the dough case. Sprinkle first with cinnamon then with raisins, and finally with the brown sugar.

5 Roll out a thin rope shape using about one-third of the remaining dough, and place around the edge of the tart. Roll the remainder into thin ropes and arrange in a lattice over the top, 4 or 5 strips in each direction, attaching to the strip around the edge.

6 Bake in a preheated oven for about 50 minutes until golden. Remove from the oven and leave to cool. Serve warm or chilled, dredged with sifted confectioners' sugar.

STEP 3

STEP 4

STEP 5

STEP 1

STEP 2

STEP 4

STEP 5

RICOTTA ICE CREAM

Ice cream is one of the traditional dishes of Italy. Everyone eats it and there are numerous **gelato** *stalls selling a wide variety of flavors, usually in a cone. It is also served sliced, as in this classic from Sicily.*

SERVES 4–6

1/4 cup pistachio nuts
1/4 cup walnuts or pecan nuts
1/4 cup toasted chopped hazelnuts
grated rind of 1 orange
grated rind of 1 lemon
2 tbsp candied ginger
2 tbsp candied cherries
1/4 cup no-need-to-soak dried apricots
2 tbsp raisins
1 1/2 cups Ricotta cheese
2 tbsp Maraschino, Amaretto, or brandy
1 tsp vanilla extract
4 egg yolks
1/2 cup superfine sugar

TO DECORATE:
whipped cream
few candied cherries, pistachio nuts, or mint
  leaves

1 Roughly chop the pistachio nuts and walnuts and mix with the hazelnuts and orange and lemon rinds. Finely chop the ginger, cherries, apricots, and raisins and add to the bowl.

2 Mix the Ricotta evenly through the fruit mixture, then beat in the liqueur and vanilla extract.

3 Put the egg yolks and sugar in a bowl and beat hard until very thick and creamy – they may be whipped over a saucepan of slowly simmering water to speed up the process. Let cool, if necessary.

4 Carefully fold the Ricotta mixture evenly through the whipped eggs and sugar until smooth.

5 Line a 7 × 5-in. bread pan with a double layer of plastic wrap or baking parchment. Pour in the Ricotta mixture, level the top, cover with more plastic wrap or baking parchment, and freeze until firm – at least overnight.

6 To serve, carefully remove the ice cream from the pan and peel off the lining. Stand on a serving dish and if liked, decorate with whipped cream using a pastry bag and star tip, and candied cherries and/or pistachio nuts. Serve in slices, with mint leaves, if liked.

FIRST COURSES

•

PASTA WITH MEAT SAUCES

•

PASTA WITH FISH SAUCES

•

PASTA & VEGETABLE DISHES

2
_
**PASTA
DISHES**

CHAPTER SIX

First Courses

Pasta dishes perfectly fulfil the requirements of an opening course – to give family and friends an immediate feeling of well-being, to delight the eye and excite the palate. This is the time to serve clear but hearty soups contrasting the colors, textures, and flavors of crisp, fresh vegetables and short pasta shapes; for a burst of mingled flavors such as those of roasted vegetables or spicy sausage, and for subtle, creamy sauces with herbs and nuts.

Serve the first course in the prettiest dishes you have, in scallop shells, or on glass plates. Serve hot dishes piping hot, cold ones refreshingly, tinglingly cold. Garnish each one with a leaf or a sprig or two of herbs, and serve them with a choice of breads in the Mediterranean style: long, crisp grissini breadsticks, olive ciabatta bread, or warm Italian loaves.

Opposite: *An Italian fisherman and his wife inspect the nets. A wide variety of fish and shellfish are caught in the seas around the Italian coast, and this abundance is reflected in the antipasti, which often include fish soups and seafood salads.*

HARICOT BEAN & PASTA SOUP

A dish with proud Mediterranean origins, this soup is a winter warmer, to be served with warm, crusty bread and, if you like, a slice of cheese.

STEP 1

STEP 2

STEP 3

STEP 4

SERVES 4

generous 1 cup dried haricot beans, soaked, drained, and rinsed (see below)
4 tbsp olive oil
2 large onions, sliced
3 garlic cloves, chopped
1 5-oz can chopped tomatoes
1 tsp dried oregano
1 tsp tomato paste
3$\frac{1}{2}$ cups water
3 oz small pasta shapes, such as fusilli or conchigliette
4 oz sun-dried tomatoes in oil, drained and sliced thinly
1 tbsp chopped fresh cilantro or flat-leaf parsley
2 tbsp grated Parmesan cheese
salt and pepper

1 Put the soaked beans into a large saucepan, cover with cold water, and bring them to a boil. Boil rapidly for 15 minutes to remove any harmful toxins. Drain the beans in a colander.

2 Heat the oil in a saucepan over a medium heat and fry the onions until they are just beginning to change color. Stir in the garlic and cook for 1 minute. Stir in the chopped tomatoes, oregano, and the tomato paste and pour on the water. Add the beans, bring to a boil, and cover the saucepan. Simmer for 45 minutes or until the beans are almost tender.

3 Add the pasta, season the soup, and stir in the sun-dried tomatoes. Return the soup to a boil, partly cover, and continue boiling for 10 minutes until the pasta is nearly tender.

4 Stir in the chopped herb. Taste the soup and adjust the seasoning if necessary. Transfer to a warmed soup tureen to serve, sprinkled with the Parmesan cheese. Serve hot.

DRIED BEANS

You can soak the dried beans for several hours or overnight in a large bowl of cold water, or, if it is more convenient, place them in a saucepan of cold water and bring them to a boil. Remove from the heat and leave the beans to cool in the water. Drain and rinse the beans before beginning the recipe.

STEP 2

STEP 3

STEP 4

STEP 5

CHICKEN SCALLOPS

Served in scallop shells, this makes a stylish presentation for a dinner-party first course.

SERVES 4

6 oz short-cut macaroni or other
   short pasta shapes
3 tbsp vegetable oil, plus extra for brushing
1 onion, chopped finely
3 slices unsmoked bacon, rinds removed and
   chopped
4 oz button mushrooms, sliced thinly or
   chopped
¾ cup cooked chicken, diced
¾ cup crème fraîche
4 tbsp dry bread crumbs
½ cup grated Cheddar cheese
salt and pepper
fresh flat-leaf parsley sprigs, to garnish

1 Cook the pasta in a large saucepan of boiling salted water, adding 1 tablespoon of the oil. When the pasta is almost tender, drain in a colander. Return to the saucepan and cover.

2 Heat the broiler to medium. Heat the remaining oil in a sauce over medium heat and fry the onion until it is translucent. Add the chopped bacon and mushrooms and cook for 3–4 minutes longer, stirring once or twice.

3 Stir in the pasta, chicken, and crème fraîche and season.

4 Brush 4 large scallop shells with oil. Spoon in the chicken mixture and smooth to make neat mounds.

5 Mix together the bread crumbs and cheese and sprinkle over the top of the chicken mixture. Press the topping lightly into the chicken mixture, then broil for 4–5 minutes until golden brown and bubbling. Garnish with parsley, and serve hot.

VARIATION

If you do not have scallop shells, you can assemble this dish in four small ovenproof dishes, such as ramekins, or in one large one. Look in good kitchen supply stores for ovenproof scallop-shaped dishes.

STEP 1

STEP 2

STEP 3

STEP 4

SPICY SAUSAGE SALAD

A warm sausage and pasta dressing spooned over chilled salad leaves makes a refreshing combination to start a meal with.

SERVES 4

4 oz small pasta shapes, such as elbow
    tubetti
3 tbsp olive oil
1 onion, chopped
2 cloves garlic, crushed
1 small yellow bell pepper, cored, deseeded,
    and cut into julienne strips
6 oz spicy pork sausage, such as pepperoni,
    skinned and sliced
2 tbsp red wine
1 tbsp red-wine vinegar
mixed salad leaves, chilled
salt

1 Cook the pasta in a large saucepan of boiling salted water, adding 1 tablespoon of the oil. When almost tender, drain it in a colander and set aside.

2 Heat the remaining oil in a saucepan over a medium heat. Fry the onion until translucent, stir in the garlic, bell pepper, and sausage and cook for 3–4 minutes, stirring once or twice.

3 Add the wine, wine vinegar, and reserved pasta to the saucepan, stir to blend well and bring the mixture just to a boil.

4 Arrange the chilled salad leaves on 4 individual serving plates and spoon on the warm sausage and pasta mixture. Serve at once.

SPICED SAUSAGES

Italian pepperoni, flavored with chili peppers, fennel, and spices, is an ideal sausage to use for this recipe. Alternatively, try one of the many varieties of salami, usually flavored with garlic and pepper.

SPAGHETTI WITH RICOTTA CHEESE

This makes a quick and easy first course, ideal for the summer.

STEP 1

STEP 2

STEP 2

STEP 3

SERVES 4

12 oz spaghetti
3 tbsp olive oil
3 tbsp butter, cut into small pieces
2 tbsp fresh chopped flat-leaf parsley
salt

SAUCE:
1 cup freshly ground almonds
$^{1}/_{2}$ cup Ricotta cheese
large pinch grated nutmeg
large pinch ground cinnamon
$^{2}/_{3}$ cup crème fraîche
$^{1}/_{2}$ cup hot chicken stock
pepper
1 tbsp pine nuts
fresh cilantro leaves, to garnish

1 Cook the spaghetti in a large saucepan of boiling salted water, adding 1 tablespoon of the oil. When it is almost tender, drain the pasta in a colander. Return it to the pan and toss with the butter and parsley. Cover the pan and keep warm.

2 To make the sauce, mix together the ground almonds, Ricotta, nutmeg, cinnamon, and crème fraîche to make a thick paste. Gradually pour in the remaining oil, stirring constantly until it is well blended. Gradually pour in the hot stock, stirring all the time, until the sauce is smooth. Season with pepper.

3 Transfer the spaghetti to a warmed serving dish, pour on the sauce and toss well. Sprinkle each serving with pine nuts and garnish with fresh cilantro leaves. Serve warm.

TOSSING SPAGHETTI

To toss spaghetti and coat it thoroughly with a sauce or dressing, use the 2 largest forks you can find – special forks are sold in some kitchen stores just for this purpose. Holding one fork in each hand, ease the prongs under the spaghetti from each side and lift them towards the center. Repeat evenly and rhythmically until the pasta is well and truly tossed.

VEGETABLE & PASTA SALAD

*Roasted vegetables and pasta make a delicious, colorful salad,
ideal as a first course or to serve with a platter of cold meats.*

STEP 1

STEP 2

STEP 3

STEP 4

SERVES 4
OVEN: 425°F

2 small eggplants, sliced thinly
1 large onion, sliced
2 large beef-steak tomatoes, skinned and cut
    into wedges
1 red bell pepper, cored, deseeded, and sliced
1 fennel bulb, sliced thinly
2 garlic cloves, sliced
4 tbsp olive oil
6 oz small pasta shapes, such as stars
salad leaves
1/2 cup feta cheese, crumbled
a few basil leaves, torn
salt and pepper

DRESSING:
5 tbsp olive oil
juice of 1 orange
1 tsp grated orange rind
1/4 tsp paprika
4 canned anchovies, chopped finely

1 Place the sliced eggplants in a colander, sprinkle with salt, and leave for about 1 hour for the salt to draw out the bitter juices. Rinse under cold running water to remove the salt, then drain. Dry on paper towels.

2 Arrange the eggplants, onion, tomatoes, red bell pepper, fennel, and garlic in a single layer in an ovenproof dish, sprinkle on 3 tablespoons of the olive oil, and season with salt and pepper. Bake in a preheated oven, uncovered, for 45 minutes, until the vegetables begin to turn brown. Remove from the oven and set aside to cool.

3 Cook the pasta in a large saucepan of boiling salted water, adding the remaining olive oil. When the pasta is almost tender, drain it in a colander, then transfer it to a bowl.

4 To make the dressing, mix together the olive oil, orange juice, orange rinds and paprika. Stir in the finely chopped anchovies and season with pepper. Pour the dressing over the pasta while it is still hot, and toss well. Set the pasta aside to cool.

5 To assemble the salad, line a shallow serving dish with the salad leaves and arrange the cold roasted vegetables in the center. Spoon the pasta in a ring around the vegetables and scatter over the feta cheese and basil leaves. Serve at once.

Pasta with Meat Sauces

Some of the most popular and best-known pasta dishes are ones
that bring together long strands of pasta cooked *al dente*,
and a rich, hearty sauce including beef or lamb, chicken or ham.
Spaghetti Bolognese needs no introduction, and yet it is said
that there are almost as many versions of this delicious regional
dish as there are lovers of Italian food. Our version includes both
beef and bacon in a sauce enriched with beef stock and red wine.

Layered pasta dishes that are served in slices, wedges, or squares are
perfect standbys for parties and picnics, buffet meals, or informal
family occasions; children and teenagers love them. Our selection
includes creamy lasagne and pasticcio, an eggplant and pasta cake,
and an unusual meat loaf with a contrasting pasta layer; they will
all make worthy additions to your repertoire of baked pasta
favorites.

Opposite: *Verdant landscape
near Bologna, home of some
splendid hams, as well as one of
the best-known pasta sauces –
Bolognese.*

SPAGHETTI BOLOGNESE

This familiar meat sauce, also known as ragù sauce, can be used in lasagne, and in other baked dishes as well. It is so versatile that it is a good idea to make it in large quantities, and freeze some.

STEP 1

STEP 2

STEP 3

STEP 4

SERVES 4

14 oz spaghetti
1 tbsp olive oil
salt
1 tbsp butter
2 tbsp chopped fresh parsley, to garnish

RAGU SAUCE:
3 tbsp olive oil
3 tbsp butter
2 large onions, chopped
4 celery stalks, sliced thinly
6 oz bacon, chopped into small strips
2 garlic cloves, chopped
1 lb lean beef, ground
2 tbsp tomato paste
1 tbsp all-purpose flour
15-oz can chopped tomatoes
$^2/_3$ cup beef stock
$^2/_3$ cup red wine
2 tsp dried oregano
$^1/_2$ tsp grated nutmeg
salt and pepper

1 To make the ragù sauce: heat the oil and the butter in a large skillet over a medium heat. Add the onions, celery, and bacon pieces and fry them together for 5 minutes, stirring once or twice.

2 Stir in the garlic and ground beef and cook, stirring, until the meat has lost its redness. Lower the heat and continue cooking for a further 10 minutes, stirring occasionally.

3 Increase the heat to medium, stir in the tomato paste and the flour, and cook for 1–2 minutes. Stir in the chopped tomatoes and the beef stock and wine and bring to a boil, stirring. Season the sauce and stir in the oregano and nutmeg. Cover the pan and simmer for 45 minutes, stirring occasionally.

4 Cook the spaghetti in a large saucepan of boiling salted water, adding the olive oil. When it is almost tender, drain it in a colander, then return to the pan. Dot the spaghetti with the butter and toss thoroughly.

5 Taste the sauce and adjust the seasoning if necessary. Pour the sauce over the spaghetti and toss well. Sprinkle on the parsley to garnish and serve immediately.

STEP 1

STEP 2

STEP 4

STEP 5

STUFFED CANNELLONI

Cannelloni, the thick round pasta tubes, make perfect containers for close-textured sauces of all kinds.

SERVES 4
OVEN: 375°F

8 cannelloni tubes
1 tbsp olive oil
fresh herbs, to garnish

FILLING:
2 tbsp butter
10 oz frozen spinach, defrosted and chopped
1/2 cup Ricotta cheese
1/4 cup grated Parmesan cheese
1/4 cup chopped ham
1/4 tsp grated nutmeg
2 tbsp heavy cream
2 eggs, lightly beaten
salt and pepper

SAUCE:
2 tbsp butter
1/4 cup all-purpose flour
1 1/4 cups milk
2 bay leaves
large pinch grated nutmeg
1/4 cup grated Parmesan

1 To prepare the filling, melt the butter in a saucepan and stir in the spinach. Stir for 2–3 minutes to allow the moisture to evaporate, then remove from the heat. Stir in the cheeses and the ham. Season with nutmeg, salt, and pepper and beat in the cream and eggs to make a thick paste. Set aside to cool.

2 Cook the cannelloni in a large saucepan of boiling salted water, adding the olive oil. When almost tender, after 10–12 minutes, drain it in a colander and set aside to cool.

3 To make the sauce, melt the butter in a pan, stir in the flour, and, when it has formed a roux, gradually pour on the milk, stirring all the time. Add the bay leaves, bring to simmering point, and cook for 5 minutes. Season with nutmeg, salt, and pepper. Remove the pan from the heat and discard the bay leaves.

4 To assemble the dish, spoon the filling into a pastry bag. Pipe it into each of the cannelloni tubes.

5 Spoon a little of the sauce into a shallow baking dish. Arrange the cannelloni in a single layer, then pour over the remaining sauce. Sprinkle on the remaining Parmesan cheese and bake in a preheated oven for 40–45 minutes until the sauce is golden brown and bubbling. Serve garnished with fresh herb sprigs.

LASAGNE VERDE

The sauce in this delicious baked pasta dish is the same sauce that is served with Spaghetti Bolognese (see page 90).

SERVES 6
OVEN: 375°F

1 quantity Ragù Sauce (see page 90)
1 tbsp olive oil
8 oz lasagne verde
1 quantity Béchamel Sauce
  (see page 196)
¹/₂ cup Parmesan, grated
salt and pepper
salad or black olives, to serve

1 Begin by making the ragù sauce as described on page 90. Cook the sauce for 10–12 minutes longer than the time given, in an uncovered pan, to allow excess liquid to evaporate. To layer the sauce with lasagne, it needs to be reduced until it has the consistency of a thick paste.

2 Have ready a large pan of boiling salted water and add the olive oil. Drop the pasta sheets into the boiling water, 2 or 3 at a time, and return the water to the boil before adding further pasta sheets. If you are using fresh lasagne, cook the sheets for a total of 8 minutes. If you are using dried or partly precooked pasta, cook it according to the directions given on the packet.

3 Spread a large, dampened dish cloth on a counter. Lift out the pasta sheets with a perforated spoon and spread them in a single layer on the dish cloth. Use a second dish cloth if necessary. Set the pasta aside while you make the béchamel sauce, as described on page 196.

4 Grease a rectangular ovenproof dish, about 10–11 in. long. To assemble the dish, spoon a little of the meat sauce into the prepared dish, cover with a layer of lasagne, then spoon over a little béchamel sauce and sprinkle on a little cheese. Continue making layers in this way, covering the final layer of lasagne with the remaining béchamel sauce.

5 Sprinkle on the remaining cheese and bake in a preheated oven for 40 minutes until the sauce is golden brown and bubbling. Serve with a chilled green salad, a tomato salad, or a bowl of black olives.

STEP 2

STEP 3

STEP 4

STEP 4

LAYERED MEAT LOAF

*A cheesy pasta layer comes as a pleasant surprise inside
this lightly spiced meat loaf.*

STEP 2

STEP 5

STEP 5

STEP 6

SERVES 6
OVEN: 350°F

2 tbsp butter, plus extra for greasing
1 onion, chopped finely
1 small red bell pepper, cored, deseeded and
    chopped
1 garlic clove, chopped
1 lb lean beef, ground
$\frac{1}{2}$ cup soft white bread crumbs
$\frac{1}{2}$ tsp chopped chili pepper
1 tbsp lemon juice
$\frac{1}{2}$ tsp grated lemon rind
2 tbsp chopped fresh flat-leaf parsley
3 oz short pasta, such as fusilli
1 tbsp olive oil
1 quantity Cheese Sauce (see pages 196–7)
4 bay leaves
6 oz bacon slices, rinds removed
salt and pepper
salad leaves, to garnish

1 Melt the butter in a pan over a medium heat and fry the onion and bell pepper for about 3 minutes, until the onion is translucent. Stir in the garlic and cook for a further 1 minute.

2 Put the meat into a large bowl and mash it with a wooden spoon until it becomes a sticky paste. Tip in the fried vegetables and stir in the bread crumbs, chili pepper, lemon juice, lemon rind, and parsley. Season the mixture with salt and pepper and set it aside.

3 Cook the pasta in a large pan of boiling salted water, adding the olive oil. When it is almost tender, drain it in a colander.

4 Make the Cheese Sauce as described on pages 196–7. Stir in the pasta.

5 Grease a 2 lb loaf pan and arrange the bay leaves in the base. Stretch the bacon slices with the back of a knife blade and arrange them to line the base and sides of the pan. Spoon in half the meat mixture, level the surface, and cover with the pasta. Spoon in the remaining meat mixture, level the top, and cover the pan with foil.

6 Cook in a preheated oven for 1 hour or until the juices run clear and the loaf has shrunk from the sides. Pour off any excess fat from the pan and turn the loaf out on to a warmed serving dish. Serve hot, garnished with salad leaves.

EGGPLANT CAKE

Layers of toasty-brown eggplant, meat sauce and cheese-flavored pasta make this a popular family supper dish.

STEP 2

STEP 3

STEP 5

STEP 6

SERVES 4
OVEN: 375°F

1 eggplant, sliced thinly
5 tbsp olive oil
1 quantity Lamb Sauce (see page 197)
8 oz short pasta shapes, such as fusilli
¼ cup butter, plus extra for greasing
6 tbsp all-purpose flour
1¼ cups milk
⅔ cup light cream
⅔ cup chicken stock
large pinch grated nutmeg
¾ cup grated Cheddar cheese
¼ cup grated Parmesan cheese
salt and pepper

1 Put the eggplant slices in a colander, sprinkle with salt, and leave for about 45 minutes while the salt draws out some of the bitter juices. Rinse the eggplant under cold running water and drain. Toss in paper towels to dry.

2 Heat 4 tablespoons of the oil in a skillet over a medium heat. Fry the eggplant slices for about 4 minutes on each side, until light golden. Remove with a perforated spoon and drain on paper towels.

3 Make the lamb sauce as described on page 197 and keep warm.

4 Meanwhile, cook the pasta in a large pan of boiling salted water, adding 1 tablespoon of olive oil. When the pasta is almost tender, drain it in a colander and return to the pan. Cover and keep warm.

5 Melt the butter in a small pan, stir in the flour, and cook for 1 minute. Gradually pour on the milk, stirring all the time, then stir in the cream and chicken stock. Season with nutmeg, salt, and pepper, bring to a boil and simmer for 5 minutes. Stir in the Cheddar and remove the pan from the heat. Pour half the sauce over the pasta and mix well. Reserve the remaining sauce.

6 Grease a shallow ovenproof dish. Spoon in half the pasta, cover it with half the lamb sauce, and then with the eggplant in a single layer. Repeat the layers of pasta and meat sauce and spread the remaining cheese sauce over the top. Sprinkle on the Parmesan. Bake in a preheated oven for 25 minutes, until the top is golden brown. Serve hot or cold, with an artichoke heart and tomato salad.

PASTICCIO

A recipe that has both Italian and Greek origins, this dish may be served hot or cold, cut into thick, satisfying squares.

STEP 1

SERVES 6
OVEN: 375°F

8 oz fusilli, or other short pasta shapes
1 tbsp olive oil
4 tbsp heavy cream
salt
fresh rosemary sprigs, to garnish

SAUCE:
2 tbsp olive oil, plus extra for brushing
1 onion, sliced thinly
1 red bell pepper, cored, deseeded, and
   chopped
2 garlic cloves, chopped
1¼ lb lean beef, ground
1 5-oz can chopped tomatoes
½ cup dry white wine
2 tbsp chopped fresh flat-leaf parsley
2-oz can anchovies, drained and chopped
salt and pepper

TOPPING:
1¼ cups natural yogurt
3 eggs
pinch grated nutmeg
⅓ cup grated Parmesan cheese

1 To make the sauce, heat the oil in a large skillet and fry the onion and red bell pepper for 3 minutes. Stir in the garlic and cook for 1 minute more. Stir in the beef and cook, stirring frequently, until it has changed color.

2 Add the tomatoes and wine, stir well, and bring to a boil. Simmer, uncovered, for 20 minutes until the sauce is fairly thick. Stir in the parsley and anchovies and adjust the seasoning.

3 Cook the pasta in a large saucepan of boiling salted water, adding the oil. When it is almost tender, drain it in a colander, then transfer it to a bowl. Stir in the cream and set it aside.

4 To make the topping, beat together the yogurt, eggs, nutmeg, and salt and pepper. Stir in half the cheese.

5 Brush a shallow baking dish with oil. Spoon in half the pasta and cover with half the meat sauce. Repeat these layers, spread the topping over evenly and sprinkle on remaining cheese.

6 Bake in a preheated oven for 25 minutes until the topping is golden brown and bubbling. Garnish with rosemary and serve with a selection of raw vegetable crudités.

STEP 2

STEP 4

STEP 5

STEP 1

STEP 2

STEP 2

STEP 3

TAGLIATELLE WITH MEATBALLS

There is an appetizing contrast of textures and flavors in this satisfying family dish.

SERVES 4

1 lb lean beef, ground
1 cup soft white bread crumbs
1 garlic clove, crushed
2 tbsp chopped fresh flat-leaf parsley
1 tsp dried oregano
large pinch grated nutmeg
$\frac{1}{4}$ tsp ground coriander
$\frac{1}{2}$ cup grated Parmesan cheese
2–3 tbsp milk
all-purpose flour for dredging
4 tbsp olive oil
14 oz tagliatelle
2 tbsp butter, diced
salt
2 tbsp chopped flat-leaf parsley, to garnish

SAUCE:
3 tbsp olive oil
2 large onions, sliced
2 celery stalks, sliced thinly
2 garlic cloves, chopped
1 5-oz can chopped tomatoes
4 oz sun-dried tomatoes in oil, drained and
   chopped
2 tbsp tomato paste
1 tbsp dark Muscovado sugar
$\frac{2}{3}$ cup white wine or water
salt and pepper

1 To make the sauce, heat the oil in a skillet and fry the onion and celery until translucent. Add the garlic and cook for 1 minute. Stir in the tomatoes, tomato paste, sugar, and wine and season. Boil and simmer for 10 minutes.

2 Break up the meat in a bowl with a wooden spoon until it becomes a sticky paste. Stir in the bread crumbs, garlic, herbs, and spices. Stir in the cheese and enough milk to make a firm paste. Flour your hands, take large spoonfuls of the mixture and shape it into 12 balls. Heat 3 tablespoons of the oil in a saucepan and fry the meatballs for 5–6 minutes until browned.

3 Pour the tomato sauce over the meatballs. Lower the heat, cover the pan, and simmer for 30 minutes, turning once or twice. Add a little extra water if the sauce begins to dry.

4 Cook the pasta in a large saucepan of boiling salted water, adding the remaining oil. When almost tender, drain it, then turn into a warmed serving dish, dot with the butter, and toss with 2 forks. Spoon the meatballs and sauce over the pasta and sprinkle on the parsley. Serve with a green salad.

CHAPTER EIGHT

Pasta with Fish Sauces

Macaroni with mushrooms and shrimp or calamares; whole wheat
lasagne with smoked fish and shrimp; pasta shells with mussels;
spaghetti with smoked salmon or with anchovies and tuna;
vermicelli with clams – these are irresistible combinations that have
a whiff of the sea and, in most cases, the flavor of the
Mediterranean.

These dishes are as practical as they are delicious, all perfect
choices for the busy cook who has to keep an eye on the clock.
In general, since fish and shellfish need only the briefest
of cooking times, the sauce and the pasta can be ready together,
perfectly cooked and perfectly timed just as the family
is assembling or the guests are arriving.

Opposite: *Open-air restaurant
beside Lake Garda. The many
rivers and lakes in Italy are a
rich source of fish and shellfish,
which feature largely in pasta
sauces.*

MACARONI & SHRIMP BAKE

This adaptation of an 18th-century Italian dish is baked until it is golden brown and sizzling, then cut into wedges, like a cake.

STEP 2

STEP 3

STEP 4

STEP 4

SERVES 4
OVEN: 350°F

12 oz short pasta, such as short-cut macaroni
1 tbsp olive oil, plus extra for brushing
6 tbsp butter, plus extra for greasing
2 small fennel bulbs, sliced thinly, leaves reserved
6 oz mushrooms, sliced thinly
6 oz peeled shrimp
Béchamel Sauce (see page 196)
pinch chili powder
¹/₂ cup grated Parmesan cheese
2 large tomatoes, sliced
1 tsp dried oregano
salt and pepper

1 Cook the pasta in a large pan of boiling salted water, adding 1 tablespoon of olive oil. When the pasta is almost tender, drain it in a colander, return to the pan, and dot with 2 tablespoons of the butter. Shake the pan well, cover tightly, and keep the pasta warm.

2 Melt the remaining butter in a pan over a medium heat and fry the fennel for 3–4 minutes until it begins to soften. Stir in the mushrooms and fry for a further 2 minutes. Stir in the shrimp, remove the pan from the heat, and set it aside.

3 Make the béchamel sauce and add the chili powder. Remove the pan from the heat and stir in the reserved vegetables and shrimp and the pasta.

4 Grease a round, shallow ovenproof dish. Pour in the pasta mixture and spread it out evenly. Sprinkle on the Parmesan and arrange the tomato slices in a ring around the edge of the dish. Brush the tomato with olive oil and sprinkle on the dried oregano.

5 Bake in a preheated oven for 25 minutes, until the top is golden brown. Serve hot.

ACCOMPANIMENT

A mixed green salad, tossed with the reserved fennel leaves and sprinkled with crumbled feta cheese, goes well with this dish.

SEAFOOD LASAGNE

Layers of cheese sauce, smoked cod and whole wheat lasagne can be assembled in advance and left ready to cook on the following day.

STEP 2

SERVES 6
OVEN: 375°F

8 sheets whole wheat lasagne
1 lb smoked cod
2¹/₂ cups milk
1 tbsp lemon juice
8 peppercorns
2 bay leaves
a few sprigs fresh flat-leaf parsley
¹/₂ cup grated Cheddar cheese
¹/₄ cup grated Parmesan cheese
salt and pepper
a few whole shrimp, to garnish (optional)

SAUCE:
¹/₄ cup butter, plus extra for greasing
1 large onion, sliced
1 green bell pepper, cored, deseeded, and
    chopped
1 small zucchini, sliced
¹/₂ cup all-purpose flour
²/₃ cup white wine
²/₃ cup light cream
4 oz shrimp
¹/₂ cup grated Cheddar cheese

1 Cook the lasagne in boiling salted water until almost tender. Drain in a colander and reserve.

2 Place the smoked cod, milk, lemon juice, peppercorns, bay leaves and parsley in a skillet. Bring to a boil, cover and simmer for 10 minutes.

3 Remove the fish, skin it, and remove any bones. Flake the fish. Strain and reserve the liquid.

4 Make the sauce: melt the butter and fry the onion, bell pepper and zucchini for 2–3 minutes. Stir in the flour and cook for 1 minute. Gradually add the fish liquid, then stir in the wine, cream and shrimp. Simmer for 2 minutes. Remove from the heat, add the cheese, and season.

5 Grease a shallow ovenproof dish. Pour in a quarter of the sauce and spread over the base. Cover the sauce with 3 sheets of lasagne, then with another quarter of the sauce. Arrange the fish on top, then cover with half the remaining sauce. Add the remaining lasagne, then remaining sauce. Sprinkle the Cheddar and Parmesan over.

6 Bake in a preheated oven for 25 minutes, or until the top is golden brown and bubbling. Garnish with a few whole shrimp, if liked.

STEP 4

STEP 5

STEP 5

PASTA SHELLS WITH MUSSELS

Serve this aromatic seafood dish to family and friends who admit to a love of garlic!

STEP 1

STEP 2

STEP 3

STEP 5

SERVES 4–6

14 oz pasta shells
1 tbsp olive oil

SAUCE:
6 pints mussels, scrubbed
2 large onions, chopped
1 cup dry white wine
¹/₂ cup unsalted butter
6 large garlic cloves, chopped finely
5 tbsp chopped fresh flat-leaf parsley
1¹/₄ cups heavy cream
salt and pepper

1 Pull off the "beards" from the mussels and rinse the mussels well in several changes of water, discarding any that refuse to close when tapped. Put the mussels in a large saucepan with one of the onions and the white wine. Cover the saucepan, shake, and cook over a medium heat for 2–3 minutes until the mussels open.

2 Remove the saucepan from the heat, lift out the mussels with a perforated spoon, reserving the liquid, and set aside until they are cool enough to handle. Discard any mussels that have not opened.

3 Melt the butter in a saucepan over a medium heat and fry the remaining onion until translucent. Stir in the garlic and cook for 1 minute. Gradually pour on the reserved cooking liquid, stirring to blend thoroughly. Stir in the parsley and cream, season, and bring to simmering point. Taste and adjust the seasoning if necessary.

4 Cook the pasta in a large saucepan of boiling salted water, adding the oil. When it is almost tender, drain it in a colander. Return the pasta to the saucepan, cover and keep warm.

5 Remove the mussels from their shells, reserving a few for garnish. Stir the mussels into the cream sauce. Tip the pasta into a warmed serving dish, pour on the sauce, and, using 2 large spoons, toss it well. Garnish with a few mussel shells. Serve hot, with warm, crusty bread.

PASTA SHELLS

Pasta shells, from medium-sized to giant ones, are ideal for this dish, because the rich, buttery sauce collects in the cavities and impregnates the pasta with the flavors of the shellfish and wine.

STEP 1

STEP 2

STEP 3

STEP 3

SPAGHETTI WITH SMOKED SALMON

*Made in moments, this is a dish to astonish and delight
unexpected guests.*

SERVES 4

1 lb buckwheat spaghetti
2 tbsp olive oil
$^1/_2$ cup crumbled feta cheese
salt
fresh cilantro, to garnish

SAUCE:
$1^1/_4$ cups heavy cream
$^2/_3$ cup whisky or brandy
4 oz smoked salmon
large pinch chili powder
2 tbsp chopped cilantro or fresh flat-leaf
     parsley
pepper

1 Cook the spaghetti in a large
saucepan of boiling salted water,
adding 1 tablespoon of the olive oil.
When the pasta is almost tender, drain it
in a colander. Return to the saucepan
and sprinkle on the remaining oil. Cover
and shake the saucepan and keep warm.

2 In separate small saucepans, heat
the cream and the whisky or
brandy to simmering point, but do not let
them boil.

3 Combine the cream and whisky or
brandy. Cut the smoked salmon
into thin strips and add to the cream.
Season with pepper and chili powder and
stir in the chopped fresh herb.

4 Transfer the spaghetti to a warmed
serving dish, pour on the sauce,
and toss thoroughly using 2 large forks.
Scatter the crumbled cheese over the
pasta and garnish with cilantro leaves.
Serve at once.

ACCOMPANIMENTS

A green salad with a lemony dressing is a
good accompaniment to this rich and
luxurious dish.

VERMICELLI WITH CLAM SAUCE

Another cook-in-a-hurry recipe that transforms storecupboard ingredients into a dish with style.

SERVES 4

14 oz vermicelli, spaghetti, or other long
  pasta
1 tbsp olive oil
2 tbsp butter
2 tbsp grated Parmesan cheese
fresh basil sprigs, to garnish

SAUCE:
1 tbsp olive oil
2 onions, chopped
2 garlic cloves, chopped
7-oz jar clams in brine
½ cup white wine
4 tbsp chopped fresh flat-leaf parsley
½ tsp dried oregano
pinch grated nutmeg
salt and pepper

1 Cook the pasta in a large saucepan of boiling salted water, adding the olive oil. When it is almost tender, drain it in a colander, return to the pan, and add the butter. Cover the saucepan. Shake it and keep it warm.

2 To make the clam sauce, heat the oil in a saucepan over a medium heat and fry the onion until it is translucent. Stir in the garlic and cook for 1 minute longer.

3 Strain the liquid from one jar of clams, pour into the saucepan and add the wine. Stir well, bring to simmering point, and simmer for 3 minutes. Drain the brine from the second jar of clams and discard. Add the clams and herbs to the pan and season with pepper and nutmeg. Lower the heat and cook until the sauce is heated through.

4 Transfer the pasta to a warmed serving dish and pour on the sauce. Sprinkle on the Parmesan and garnish with the basil. Serve hot.

PARMESAN

You could use grated Parmesan for this dish, but flakes of fresh Parmesan, carved off the block, give it an added depth of flavor.

STEP 1

STEP 2

STEP 3

STEP 3

STEP 2

STEP 2

STEP 3

STEP 3

SPAGHETTI WITH TUNA & PARSLEY SAUCE

This is a recipe to look forward to when parsley is at its most prolific, in the summer growing season.

SERVES 4

1 lb spaghetti
1 tbsp olive oil
2 tbsp butter
black olives, to garnish

SAUCE:
7-oz can tuna, drained
2-oz can anchovies, drained
1 cup olive oil
1 cup roughly chopped parsley
²/₃ cup crème fraîche
salt and pepper

1 Cook the spaghetti in a large saucepan of boiling salted water, adding the olive oil. When it is almost tender, drain it in a colander and return to the saucepan. Add the butter, toss thoroughly to coat, and keep warm.

2 Remove any bones from the tuna. Put it into a blender or food processor with the anchovies, olive oil, and parsley and process until the sauce is smooth. Pour in the crème fraîche and process for a few seconds to blend. Taste the sauce and adjust the seasoning.

3 Warm 4 plates. Shake the saucepan of spaghetti over a medium heat until it is thoroughly warmed through, then transfer to a serving dish. Pour on the sauce and toss quickly, using 2 forks. Garnish with the olives and serve immediately with warm, crusty bread.

KNOW YOUR OIL

Oils produced by different countries, mainly Italy, Spain, and Greece, have their own characteristic flavors. Some olive varieties produce an oil which has a hot and peppery taste, while others, such as the Kalamata, grown in Greece, give a distinctly "green" flavor. Get to know and recognize the different grades of oil, too. Extra virgin olive oil, the finest grade, is made from the first, cold pressing of olives. Virgin olive oil, which has a fine aroma and color, is also made by cold pressing, but it may have a slightly higher acidity level than extra virgin oil. Refined or pure olive oil is made by treating the paste residue with heat or solvents to remove the residual oil. Olive oil is a blend of refined and virgin olive oil.

SQUID & MACARONI STEW

This Mediterranean dish is quick and easy to make, yet has all the authentic flavor of life beside the sea.

STEP 2

STEP 2

STEP 3

STEP 4

SERVES 4–6

8 oz short-cut macaroni or other short pasta
   shapes
1 tbsp olive oil
2 tbsp chopped fresh flat-leaf parsley
salt and pepper

SAUCE:
12 oz cleaned squid (see below)
6 tbsp olive oil
2 onions, sliced
1 cup fish stock
$^2/_3$ cup red wine
12 oz tomatoes, skinned and sliced thinly
2 tbsp tomato paste
1 tsp dried oregano
2 bay leaves

1 Cook the pasta for only 3 minutes in a large saucepan of boiling salted water, adding the oil. When it is almost tender, drain the pasta in a colander, return to the pan, cover and keep warm.

2 Cut the squid into 1½-in. strips. Heat the oil in a saucepan over a medium heat and fry the onions until translucent. Add the squid and stock and simmer for 5 minutes. Pour on the wine and add the tomatoes, tomato paste, oregano, and bay leaves. Bring the sauce to a boil, then season and cook, uncovered, for 5 minutes.

3 Add the pasta, stir well, cover the saucepan, and continue simmering for 10 minutes or until the macaroni and squid are almost tender. By this time the sauce should be thick and syrupy. If it is too liquid, uncover the pan and continue cooking for a few minutes. Taste the sauce and adjust the seasoning if necessary.

4 Remove the bay leaves and stir in most of the parsley, reserving a little to garnish. Transfer to a warmed serving dish. Sprinkle on the remaining parsley and serve hot. Serve with warm, crusty bread such as ciabatta.

CLEANING SQUID

Peel off the skin and cut off the head and tentacles. Remove the transparent bone from the body, then turn the body sac inside out and wash thoroughly. Cut off the tentacles to use and discard the head.

CHAPTER NINE

Pasta & Vegetable Dishes

Eggplant shells filled with Mozzarella and pasta shapes; crisp and crunchy vegetables like celery and bell peppers stir-fried with pasta shells and tossed in a sweet and sour sauce; a pasta omelet of just-cooked eggs flavored with onion, fennel, and garlic – this chapter takes you on a gastronomic tour through Italy.

Whether you choose to simmer vegetables lightly in water or stock, to steam them, or to stir-fry them, be sure to cook them only until they, like the pasta, are *al dente* and still slightly crisp. In this way the vegetables will retain more of their nutrients and most of their color and will contrast both appealingly and deliciously with their pasta accompaniment.

Opposite: *The rolling hills of Val d'Oreia, near Pienza, Tuscany. Much of the country's food – grains, rice, meat, fruit, and vegetables – is produced in the fertile Tuscan soil.*

STEP 1

STEP 3

STEP 5

STEP 5

BAKED PASTA & BEANS

A satisfying winter dish, this is a vegetarian version of cassoulet, a slow-cooked, one-pot meal.

SERVES 6
OVEN: 350°F

*generous 1 cup dried haricot beans, soaked
    and drained
8 oz penne or other short pasta shapes
6 tbsp olive oil
3¹/₂ cups vegetable stock
2 large onions, sliced
2 garlic cloves, chopped
2 bay leaves
1 tsp dried oregano
1 tsp dried thyme
5 tbsp red wine
2 tbsp tomato paste
2 celery stalks, sliced
1 fennel bulb, sliced
4 oz mushrooms, sliced
8 oz tomatoes, sliced
1 tsp dark Muscovado sugar
4 tbsp dry white bread crumbs
salt and pepper*

1 Put the beans in a saucepan, cover with water, and bring to a boil. Boil rapidly for 20 minutes, then drain.

2 Cook the pasta for only 3 minutes in a large saucepan of boiling salted water, adding 1 tablespoon of the oil. When almost tender, drain the pasta in a colander and set aside.

3 Place the beans in a large flameproof casserole, pour on the vegetable stock, and stir in the remaining olive oil, the onions, garlic, bay leaves, herbs, wine, and tomato paste.

4 Bring the stock to a boil, then cover the casserole and cook it in the preheated oven for 2 hours.

5 Add the reserved pasta, the celery, fennel, mushrooms, and tomatoes, and season with salt and pepper. Stir in the sugar and sprinkle the bread crumbs over. Cover the casserole and continue cooking it for 1 hour. Serve it hot, with salad leaves and plenty of crusty bread.

NOTE

Do not use a salted vegetable stock for the initial cooking stage of this dish, since the salt would inhibit the softening process of the beans as they gradually absorb the liquid.

STEP 2

STEP 3

STEP 4

STEP 6

VEGETABLE PASTA STIR-FRY

*Prepare all the vegetables and cook the pasta in advance,
then the dish can be cooked in a few minutes.*

SERVES 4

*14 oz whole wheat pasta shells or other
   short pasta shapes*
1 tbsp olive oil
2 carrots, sliced thinly
4 oz baby corn
3 tbsp peanut oil
*1-in. piece gingerroot, peeled and sliced
   thinly*
1 large onion, sliced thinly
1 garlic clove, sliced thinly
3 celery stalks, sliced thinly
*1 small red bell pepper, cored, deseeded, and
   sliced into julienne strips*
*1 small green bell pepper, cored, deseeded,
   and sliced into matchstick strips*
salt

SAUCE:
1 tsp cornstarch
2 tbsp water
3 tbsp soy sauce
3 tbsp dry sherry
1 tsp clear honey
few drops hot-pepper sauce (optional)

1 Cook the pasta in a large saucepan of boiling salted water, adding the tablespoon of olive oil. When almost tender, drain the pasta in a colander, return to the pan, cover, and keep warm.

2 Cook the sliced carrot and baby corn in boiling salted water for 2 minutes, then drain in a colander, plunge into cold water to prevent further cooking, and drain again.

3 Heat the peanut oil in a wok or a large skillet over a medium heat and fry the ginger for 1 minute, to flavor the oil. Remove with a perforated spoon and discard.

4 Add the onion, garlic, celery, and bell peppers to the oil and stir-fry for 2 minutes. Add the carrots and baby corn and stir-fry for a further 2 minutes, then stir in the reserved pasta.

5 Put the cornstarch into a small bowl and gradually pour on the water, stirring constantly. Stir in the soy sauce, sherry, and honey.

6 Pour the sauce into the wok or skillet, stir well, and cook for 2 minutes, stirring once or twice. Taste the sauce and season with hot-pepper sauce if liked. Serve with a steamed green vegetable such as snow peas.

BAKED EGGPLANT WITH PASTA

Combined with tomatoes and Mozzarella, pasta makes a great filling for baked eggplant shells.

STEP 2

SERVES 4
OVEN: 400°F

8 oz penne or other short pasta shapes
4 tbsp olive oil, plus extra for brushing
2 medium eggplants
1 large onion, chopped
2 garlic cloves, crushed
15-oz can chopped tomatoes
2 tsp dried oregano
2 oz Mozzarella cheese, sliced thinly
¼ cup grated Parmesan cheese
2 tbsp dry bread crumbs
salt and pepper

1 Cook the pasta in a large saucepan of boiling salted water, adding 1 tablespoon of the olive oil. When it is almost tender, drain the pasta in a colander, return to the pan, cover, and keep warm.

2 Cut the eggplants in half lengthwise. Score around the inside with a knife, then scoop out the flesh with a spoon, taking care not to pierce the skin. Brush the insides of the eggplant shells with olive oil. Chop the eggplant flesh and set it aside.

3 Heat the remaining oil in a skillet over a medium heat and fry the onion until it is translucent. Add the garlic and fry for 1 minute. Add the chopped eggplants and fry for 5 minutes, stirring frequently. Add the tomatoes and oregano and season with salt and pepper. Bring to a boil and simmer for 10 minutes or until the mixture is thick. Taste and adjust the seasoning if necessary. Remove from the heat and stir in the reserved pasta.

4 Brush a cookie sheet with oil and arrange the eggplant shells in a single layer. Divide half the tomato mixture between the 4 shells. Arrange the Mozzarella on top and cover with the remaining mixture, piling it into a mound. Mix together the Parmesan and bread crumbs, then sprinkle over the top, patting it lightly into the mixture.

5 Bake in a preheated oven for 25 minutes until the topping is golden brown. Serve hot, with a green salad.

STEP 3

STEP 4

STEP 4

STEP 2

STEP 3

STEP 3

STEP 5

VERMICELLI PIE

Lightly cooked vermicelli is pressed into a pie pan and baked with a creamy mushroom filling.

SERVES 4
OVEN: 350°F

8 oz vermicelli or spaghetti
1 tbsp olive oil
2 tbsp butter, plus extra for greasing
salt

SAUCE:
$^1/_4$ cup butter
1 onion, chopped
5 oz button mushrooms, trimmed
1 green bell pepper, cored, deseeded, and
    sliced into thin rings
$^2/_3$ cup milk
3 eggs, lightly beaten
2 tbsp heavy cream
1 tsp dried oregano
pinch grated nutmeg
pepper
1 tbsp grated Parmesan cheese

1 Cook the pasta in a large saucepan of boiling salted water, adding olive oil. When almost tender, drain it in a colander. Return to the pan, add the butter, and shake the pan.

2 Grease an 8-in. loose-bottom pie pan. Press the pasta on the base and round the sides to form a case.

3 Heat the butter in a skillet over a medium heat and fry the onion well until it is translucent. Remove with a perforated spoon and spread it in the pie case.

4 Add the mushrooms and bell pepper rings to the pan and turn them in the fat until they are glazed. Fry them for about 2 minutes on each side, then arrange in the pie case.

5 Beat together the milk, eggs, and cream, stir in the oregano, and season with nutmeg and pepper. Pour the custard mixture carefully over the vegetables and sprinkle on the cheese.

6 Bake the pie in the preheated oven for 40–45 minutes, until the filling is set. Slide on to a serving plate and serve warm.

VARIATIONS

You can use this moist and buttery pie case with any of your favorite fillings: chopped bacon, cheese and herbs, or a mixture of diced ham and sliced mushrooms; or cooked and flaked smoked haddock with corn kernels.

STEP 3

STEP 3

STEP 3

STEP 4

PASTA OMELET

Use any leftover cooked pasta you may have, such as penne, short-cut macaroni, or shells, to make this fluffy omelet an instant success.

SERVES 2

4 tbsp olive oil
1 small Spanish onion, chopped
1 fennel bulb, sliced thinly
4 oz raw potato, diced and dried
1 garlic clove, chopped
4 eggs
1 tbsp chopped fresh flat-leaf parsley
pinch chili powder
3 oz short pasta, cooked weight
1 tbsp stuffed green olives, halved, plus extra
   to garnish
salt and pepper
fresh marjoram sprigs, to garnish

1 Heat 2 tablespoons of the oil in a heavy skillet over a low heat and fry the onion, fennel, and potato for 8–10 minutes, stirring occasionally, until the potato is just tender. Do not allow it to break up. Stir in the garlic and cook for 1 further minute. Remove the pan from the heat, lift out the vegetables with a perforated spoon, and set aside. Rinse and dry the pan.

2 Break the eggs into a bowl and beat them until they are frothy. Stir in the parsley and season with salt, pepper, and chili powder.

3 Heat 1 tablespoon of the remaining oil in a skillet over a medium heat. Pour in half the beaten eggs, then add the cooked vegetables, the pasta, and the olives. Pour on the remaining egg and cook until the sides begin to set.

4 Lift up the edges with a spatula to allow the uncooked egg to spread underneath. Continue cooking the omelet, shaking the skillet occasionally, until the underside is golden brown.

5 Slide the omelet out on to a large, flat plate and wipe the skillet clean with paper towels. Heat the remaining oil in the skillet and invert the omelet. Cook on the other side until it is also golden brown.

6 Slide the omelet onto a warmed serving dish. Garnish with a few olives and fresh marjoram, and serve hot, cut into wedges, with a tomato salad.

3

PIZZAS

CHAPTER TEN

Basics

The success of a pizza depends on the quality of the bread dough base and the tomato sauce. A homemade bread dough base topped with a delicious freshly made tomato sauce will give you the closest thing possible to an authentic Italian pizza in your own kitchen. If time is short and you cannot wait for the dough to rise, make either a biscuit or a potato base. Alternatively, ready-made bases or pizza-base mixes can suffice, but these do not provide the same aroma of home-baked bread, nor the sense of achievement.

Choose tomatoes that are canned in juice rather than water, as these make a thicker sauce. Many brands of chopped tomatoes have added ingredients such as garlic, chili, onion, basil, and mixed herbs, which will add extra flavor to your tomato sauces. For pizza fans and busy cooks, make double the quantity of the basic bread dough and freeze the dough that is not required after it has been kneaded. Or you can roll out the dough in the usual way, arrange the topping on it, and bake for 10 minutes, then cool and freeze. Reheat by cooking from frozen for 15 minutes. The tomato sauces also freeze well, so make up large quantities and freeze the excess, and then you can have pizzas whenever you wish.

Opposite: The many-levelled red tile roofs and deep green trees of a typical Italian hill town.

STEP 3

STEP 4

STEP 5

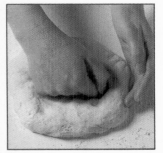

STEP 6

BREAD DOUGH BASE

Traditionally, pizza bases are made from bread dough; this recipe will give you a base similar to an Italian pizza. Always use all-purpose flour which can be white, whole wheat, or a combination of both.

MAKES ONE 10-INCH ROUND

$^1/_2$-oz cake compressed yeast or 1 tsp dried or
  easy-blend yeast
7 tbsp tepid water
$^1/_2$ tsp sugar
1 tbsp olive oil
$1^1/_2$ cups all-purpose flour
1 tsp salt

1 Combine the compressed yeast with the water and sugar in a bowl. If using dried yeast, sprinkle it over the surface of the water and whisk in until dissolved.

2 Let the mixture rest in a warm place for 10–15 minutes until frothy on the surface. Stir in the olive oil.

3 Sift the flour and salt into a large bowl. If using easy-blend yeast, stir it in at this point. Make a well in the center and pour in the yeast liquid, or water and oil (without the sugar for easy-blend yeast).

4 Using floured hands or a wooden spoon, mix together to form a dough. Turn out on to a floured counter and knead for about 5 minutes until smooth and elastic.

5 Place in a large greased plastic bag and leave in a warm place for about 1 hour or until doubled in size. (Airing closets are good places for this, as the temperature remains constant.)

6 Turn out on to a lightly floured counter and punch down by punching the dough. This releases any air bubbles which would make the pizza uneven. Knead 4 or 5 times. The dough is now ready to use.

FREEZING

Pizza dough can be frozen after the first kneading. Wrap in plastic wrap and label with the date and quantity before freezing. Defrost at room temperature and let rise in the usual way. Continue as from step 5.

STEP 2

STEP 3

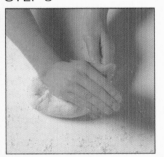

STEP 4

STEP 5

BISCUIT BASE

This is a quick and easy alternative to the bread dough base. If you do not have time to wait for bread dough to rise, a biscuit base is the next best thing.

MAKES ONE 10-IN. ROUND

1¹/₂ cups self-rising flour
¹/₂ tsp salt
2 tbsp butter, diced
¹/₂ cup milk

1 Sift the flour and salt into a large mixing bowl.

2 Rub in the butter with your fingertips until the mixture resembles fine bread crumbs.

3 Make a well in the center of the flour and butter mixture and pour in nearly all the milk at once. Mix in quickly with a knife. Add the remaining milk only if needed to make a soft dough.

4 Turn the dough out onto a floured counter and knead by turning and pressing with the heel of your hand 3 or 4 times.

5 Either roll out or press the dough into a 10-in. round on a lightly greased cookie sheet or pizza pan. Push up the edge all round slightly to form a ridge and use immediately.

ADDING TASTE

You can vary the taste of your biscuit base by adding a little grated cheese or ¹/₂ teaspoon dried oregano or mixed herbs to it for a more interesting flavor. Add your extra flavorings to the mixture after rubbing in the butter.

RUBBING IN

When rubbing in butter, it helps if your hands and the butter are very cold. Cut the butter into small dice first, then cut it into the flour with 2 knives held like scissors. Finally, rub in the remaining lumps of butter with your fingertips, remembering to keep your hands cool as you go.

POTATO BASE

This is an unusual pizza base made from mashed potatoes and flour and is a great way to use up any leftover boiled potatoes. Children love this base and you will soon have them asking for more.

STEP 1

STEP 2

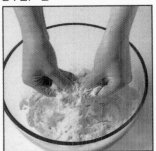

STEP 3

STEP 4

MAKES ONE 10-IN. ROUND

8 oz boiled potatoes
4 tbsp butter or margarine
1 cup self-rising flour
¹/₂ tsp salt

1 If the potatoes are hot, mash them, then stir in the butter until it has melted and is distributed evenly throughout the potatoes. Let cool.

2 Sift the flour and salt together, stir into the mashed potato mixture, and mix together to form a soft dough.

3 If the potatoes are cold, mash them without adding the butter. Sift the flour and salt into a bowl. Rub in the butter with your fingertips until the mixture resembles fine bread crumbs, then stir the flour and butter mixture into the mashed potatoes to form a soft dough.

4 Either roll out or press the dough into a 10-in. round on a lightly greased cookie sheet or pizza pan, pushing up the edge all round slightly to form a ridge before adding the topping. This base is tricky to lift before it is cooked, so you will find it easier to handle

if you roll it out directly on the cookie sheet.

5 If the base is not required for cooking immediately, you can cover it with plastic wrap and chill it for up to 2 hours.

USING INSTANT COOKED POTATOES

If time is short and you do not have any leftover cooked potatoes, make up a batch of instant dried mashed potato, keeping the consistency fairly dry, and use that instead – it will work just as well.

EXTRA FLAVOR

To add more flavor to this base, you can include dried or fresh herbs, fried chopped onion, grated cheese, or even a grated carrot. Any of these will add a delicious subtle taste to your pizza base.

TOMATO SAUCE

Use cans of either chopped or whole plum tomatoes for this sauce.
Many cooks prefer to use chopped tomatoes as it saves time, and the
plum tomatoes tend to be on the watery side. For a really spicy sauce,
add a chopped fresh red chili when frying the onions.

STEP 1

MAKES ENOUGH TO COVER ONE
10-IN. PIZZA BASE

1 small onion, chopped
1 garlic clove, crushed
1 tbsp olive oil
7-oz can chopped tomatoes
2 tsp tomato paste
½ tsp sugar
½ tsp dried oregano
1 bay leaf
salt and pepper

STEP 2

1 Fry the onion and garlic slowly in the oil for 5 minutes until softened but not browned.

2 Add the tomatoes, tomato paste, sugar, oregano, bay leaf, and seasoning. Stir well.

3 Bring to a boil, then cover and simmer slowly for 20 minutes, stirring occasionally, until you have a thickish sauce.

4 Remove the bay leaf and adjust the seasoning to taste. Let cool completely before using. This sauce keeps well in a screw-top jar in the refrigerator for up to 1 week.

TOMATOES

Tomatoes are actually berries and are related to potatoes. There are many different shapes and sizes of this versatile fruit. The one most used in Italian cooking is the plum tomato. Large beefsteak tomatoes or small, sweet cherry tomatoes are ideal for use in accompanying salads.

USING CHILIES

Take care when chopping chilies as they can burn your skin. Handle them as little as possible – you can even wear rubber gloves if you wish. Always wash your hands thoroughly afterward, and don't touch your face or eyes before you have washed your hands.

Remove chili seeds before chopping the chilies, as they are the hottest part, and shouldn't be allowed to slip into the food.

STEP 3

STEP 4

STEP 1

STEP 2

STEP 3

STEP 4

SPECIAL TOMATO SAUCE

This sauce is made with fresh tomatoes. Use the plum variety whenever available and always choose the reddest tomatoes to give a better color and sweetness to the sauce. When fresh plum tomatoes are readily available, make several batches of sauce and freeze them.

MAKES ENOUGH TO COVER ONE
10-IN. PIZZA BASE

1 small onion, chopped
1 small red bell pepper, cored, deseeded, and
*   chopped*
1 garlic clove, crushed
2 tbsp olive oil
8 oz tomatoes
1 tbsp tomato paste
1 tsp soft brown sugar
2 tsp chopped fresh basil
1/2 tsp dried oregano
1 bay leaf
salt and pepper

1 Fry the onion, bell pepper, and garlic slowly in the oil for 5 minutes until softened but not browned.

2 Cut a cross in the base of each tomato and place them in a bowl. Pour on boiling water and leave for about 45 seconds. Drain, and then plunge in cold water. The skins will slide off easily.

3 Chop the tomatoes, discarding any hard cores. Add the chopped tomatoes, tomato paste, sugar, herbs, and seasoning to the onion mixture. Stir well. Bring to a boil, then cover and simmer slowly for 30 minutes, stirring occasionally, until you have a thickish sauce.

4 Remove the bay leaf and adjust the seasoning to taste. Let cool completely before using.

5 This sauce will keep well in a screw-top jar in the refrigerator for up to 1 week.

SKINNING TOMATOES

You can skin tomatoes in another way if you have a gas stove. Cut a cross in the base of the tomato, push it on to a fork, and hold it over a gas flame, turning it slowly so that the skin heats evenly all over. The skin will start to bubble and split, and should then slide off easily.

CHAPTER ELEVEN

Meat & Fish Pizzas

A meat or fish pizza provides a very substantial, well-balanced meal. Pizzas can be topped with almost any type of meat or fish, which can lead to many highly imaginative dishes.
As pizzas are baked in a hot oven for a fairly short time, the meat should be cooked before it is added to the pizza, or it will end up undercooked. For the best results the meat should be ground or cut into small pieces. Bacon can be added in its raw state as this is usually thinly sliced and cooks very quickly.
There are almost endless varieties of salamis, sliced cured meats, hams, sausages, and bacon, either pre-packaged or from the delicatessen counter, which make perfect pizza toppings.

Canned or fresh fish or shellfish are wonderful on pizzas. Use anything from whole fresh sprats, mussels or clams in their shells, canned sardines, and monkfish to just plain cod. The most popular fish known to the pizza are, of course, anchovies and you either love them or hate them. One of the most famous pizzas on which they are used is the Pizza Napoletana, which is found in Naples; the topping is basically anchovies and olives without any cheese. If you find anchovies too salty, it helps to soak them in a little milk before using.

Opposite: *Sunset over the Grand Canal, Venice.*

STEP 2

STEP 3

STEP 4

STEP 5

HOT CHILI BEEF

This deep-pan pizza is topped with ground beef, red kidney beans and jalapeño chilies, which are small, green and hot. Add more or less chili powder depending on taste. If you prefer a slightly stronger tasting cheese, try Wisconsin Jack.

SERVES 2–4
OVEN: 400°F

FOR THE DOUGH BASE:
¾ oz compressed yeast or 1½ tsp dried or
    easy-blend yeast
½ cup tepid water
1 tsp sugar
3 tbsp olive oil
2 cups all-purpose flour
1 tsp salt

FOR THE TOPPING:
1 small onion, sliced thinly
1 garlic clove, crushed
½ yellow bell pepper, cored, deseeded, and
    chopped
1 tbsp olive oil
6 oz lean ground beef
¼ tsp chili powder
¼ tsp ground cumin
7 oz can red kidney beans, drained
1 quantity Tomato Sauce (see page 143)
1 oz jalapeño chilies, sliced
2 oz Mozzarella cheese, sliced thinly
2 oz Monterey Jack cheese, grated
olive oil for drizzling
salt and pepper
chopped fresh flat-leaf parsley, to garnish

1 To make the deep-pan dough base, use the same method as for making the Bread Dough Base recipe (see page 136).

2 Roll out or press the dough, using a rolling pin or your hands, into a 9 in. round on a lightly floured counter. Place on a pizza pan and push up the edge to fit and form a small ridge. Cover and leave to rise slightly for about 10 minutes.

3 Fry the onion, garlic and bell pepper slowly in the oil for 5 minutes until softened but not browned. Increase the heat slightly and add the beef, chili and cumin. Fry for 5 minutes, stirring occasionally. Remove from the heat, stir in the kidney beans, and season.

4 Spread the tomato sauce over the dough almost to the edge and top with the meat mixture.

5 Top with the sliced chilies and Mozzarella and sprinkle over the grated cheese. Drizzle with a little olive oil and season.

6 Bake in a preheated oven for 18–20 minutes or until the crust is golden. Serve immediately sprinkled with chopped parsley.

STEP 1

STEP 2

STEP 3

STEP 4

SMOKY BACON & PEPPERONI

This more traditional kind of pizza is topped with pepperoni, smoked bacon and bell peppers covered with a smoked cheese.

SERVES 2–4
OVEN: 400°F

1 quantity Bread Dough Base
   (see page 136)
1 tbsp olive oil
1 tbsp grated Parmesan cheese
1 quantity Tomato Sauce (see page 143)
4 oz lightly smoked bacon, diced
1/2 green bell pepper, cored, deseeded, and
   sliced thinly
1/2 yellow bell pepper, cored, deseeded, and
   sliced thinly
2 oz pepperoni-style sliced spicy sausage
2 oz smoked Bavarian cheese, grated
1/2 tsp dried oregano
olive oil for drizzling
salt and pepper

1 Roll out or press the dough, using a rolling pin or your hands, into a 10 in. round on a lightly floured counter. Place on a large greased cookie sheet or pizza pan and push up the edge a little with your fingers to form a rim.

2 Brush the base with the olive oil and sprinkle the Parmesan over it. Cover and leave to rise slightly in a warm place for about 10 minutes.

3 Spread the tomato sauce over the base almost to the edge. Top with the bacon and bell peppers. Arrange the pepperoni slices over and sprinkle with the smoked cheese.

4 Sprinkle over the oregano and drizzle with a little olive oil. Season well.

5 Bake in a preheated oven for 18–20 minutes or until the crust is golden and crisp around the edge. Cut into wedges and serve immediately.

SAVING TIME

Pre-packaged, thinly sliced pepperoni and diced bacon can be purchased from most supermarkets, which helps to save on preparation time.

PEPPERONI

A spicy pepperoni-style sausage can be quite hot. If you prefer a milder taste, use slices of salami, chorizo, or even sliced, cooked sausages in its place.

STEP 1

STEP 3

STEP 3

STEP 4

FOUR SEASONS

This is a traditional pizza on which the toppings are divided into four sections, each of which is supposed to depict a season of the year. Sliced pepperoni, salami, or kabanos (a small, spicy sausage) can be used instead of the chorizo.

SERVES 2–4
OVEN: 400°F

1 quantity Bread Dough Base
  (see page 136)
1 quantity Special Tomato Sauce
  (see page 144)
1 oz chorizo sausage, sliced thinly
1 oz button mushrooms, wiped and
  sliced thinly
1½ oz artichoke hearts, sliced thinly
1 oz Mozzarella cheese, sliced thinly
3 anchovies, halved lengthwise
2 tsp capers
4 pitted black olives, sliced
4 fresh basil leaves, shredded
olive oil for drizzling
salt and pepper

1 Roll out or press the dough, using a rolling pin or your hands, into a 10 in. round on a lightly floured counter. Place on a large greased cookie sheet or pizza pan and push up the edge a little.

2 Cover and leave to rise slightly for 10 minutes in a warm place before spreading with tomato sauce almost to the edge.

3 Put the sliced chorizo on a quarter of the pizza, the sliced mushrooms on another, the artichoke hearts on a third, and the Mozzarella and anchovies on the fourth.

4 Dot the pizza with the capers, olives, and basil leaves. Drizzle a little olive oil over the pizza and season. Do not put any salt on the anchovy section as the fish are very salty.

5 Bake in a preheated oven for 18–20 minutes or until the crust is golden and crisp. Serve immediately.

FISHY ALTERNATIVE

Fish-lovers could make a seafood four seasons pizza using shrimp, cockles, mussels, and anchovies, with one ingredient on each quarter, placed in a decorative arrangement.

STEP 1

STEP 2

STEP 3

STEP 4

MARINARA

This pizza is topped with frozen mixed seafood such as shrimp, mussels, cockles, and squid rings. Alternatively, fresh seafood can be bought from the fresh fish counter in most supermarkets. If you prefer, you can just use peeled shrimp.

SERVES 2–4
OVEN: 400°F

1 quantity Potato Base (see page 140)
1 quantity Special Tomato Sauce
   (see page 144)
7 oz frozen seafood cocktail, defrosted
1 tbsp capers
1 small yellow bell pepper, cored, deseeded,
   and chopped
1 tbsp chopped fresh marjoram
1/2 tsp dried oregano
2 oz Mozzarella cheese, grated
1 tbsp grated Parmesan cheese
12 black olives
olive oil for drizzling
salt and pepper
sprig of fresh marjoram or oregano,
   to garnish

1 Roll out or press out the potato dough, using a rolling pin or your hands, into a 10 in. round on a lightly floured counter. Place on a large greased cookie sheet or pizza pan and push up the edge a little with your fingers to form a rim.

2 Spread with the tomato sauce almost to the edge.

3 Arrange the seafood cocktail, capers, and yellow bell pepper on the sauce.

4 Sprinkle over the herbs and cheeses. Arrange the olives on top. Drizzle over a little olive oil and season well with salt and pepper.

5 Bake in a preheated oven for 18–20 minutes until the edge of the pizza is crisp and golden.

6 Transfer to a warmed serving plate, garnish with a sprig of marjoram or oregano, and serve immediately.

SEAFOOD TOPPING

If you prefer, you can replace any of the seafood with small pieces of monkfish, lemon sole, cod, or slices of crabstick.

STEP 1

STEP 3

STEP 4

STEP 5

ALASKA PIZZA

Chunks of canned salmon top this tasty pizza. You can use either red or pink salmon. Red salmon will give a better color and flavor but it can be expensive.

SERVES 2–4
OVEN: 400°F

1 quantity Biscuit Base
  (see page 138)
1 quantity Tomato Sauce (see page 143)
1 zucchini, grated
1 tomato, sliced thinly
3¹/₂ oz can red or pink salmon
2 oz button mushrooms, wiped and sliced
1 tbsp chopped fresh dill
¹/₂ tsp dried oregano
1¹/₂ oz Mozzarella cheese, grated
olive oil for drizzling
salt and pepper
sprig of fresh dill, to garnish

1 Roll out or press the dough, using a rolling pin or your hands, into a 10 in. round on a lightly floured counter. Place on a large greased cookie sheet or pizza pan and push up the edge a little with your fingers to form a rim.

2 Spread with the tomato sauce almost to the edge.

3 Top the tomato sauce with the grated zucchini, then lay the tomato slices on top.

4 Drain the can of salmon. Remove any bones and skin and flake the fish. Arrange on the pizza with the mushrooms. Sprinkle over the herbs and cheese. Drizzle with a little olive oil and season well.

5 Bake in a preheated oven for 18–20 minutes or until the edge is golden and crisp.

6 Transfer to a warmed serving plate and serve immediately, garnished with a sprig of dill.

ECONOMY VERSION

If salmon is too expensive, use either canned tuna or sardines to make a delicious everyday fish pizza. Choose canned fish in brine for a healthier topping. If fresh dill is unavailable, you can use parsley instead.

CHAPTER TWELVE

Vegetarian Pizzas

Although this chapter is for vegetarians, anyone can enjoy these pizzas. With a little imagination there is no end to the variety of vegetarian pizzas that can be produced, and as vegetables are so full of color, they make attractive and tempting toppings. Choose the best quality fresh vegetables and herbs to give maximum flavor. Tofu and TVP (soy granules) make very good pizza toppings and they marinate particularly well. For extra flavor use a smoked tofu. Ground TVP (soy granules) can be used in place of ground meat in any pizza to make a vegetarian version.

A wide variety of antipasti are sold in jars of olive oil, such as artichoke hearts, sun-dried tomatoes, sliced bell peppers, and mushrooms, which make perfect pizza topping ingredients. Use the oil in the jar to drizzle over the pizza before baking to keep it moist. If you prefer, you can use vegetarian Cheddar or Mozzarella, which are widely available. You can substitute the vegetarian variety for the cheese suggested in most of the recipes in this section (except in the Three Cheese and Artichoke recipe on page 165) for a slightly different taste.

Opposite: *The sun sets over the lush Chianti vineyards in Tuscany.*

STEP 1

STEP 3

STEP 4

STEP 5

FLORENTINE

A pizza adaptation of Eggs Florentine – sliced hard-cooked eggs on freshly cooked spinach with a little nutmeg. The bread crumbs and almonds give the pizza topping an extra crunch.

SERVES 2–4
OVEN: 400°F

2 tbsp grated Parmesan cheese
1 quantity Potato Base (see page 140)
1 quantity Tomato Sauce (see page 143)
6 oz fresh spinach leaves
1 small red onion, sliced thinly
2 tbsp olive oil
¼ tsp freshly grated nutmeg
2 hard-cooked eggs
¼ cup fresh white bread crumbs
2 oz Jarlsberg cheese, grated
  (or Emmental, Cheddar, or Gruyère,
  if not available)
2 tbsp slivered almonds
olive oil for drizzling
salt and pepper

1 Mix the Parmesan with the potato base. Roll out or press the dough, using a rolling pin or your hands, into a 10 in. round on a lightly floured counter. Place on a large greased cookie sheet or pizza pan and push up the edge slightly. Spread with the tomato sauce almost to the edge.

2 Remove the spinach stems and wash the leaves in plenty of cold water. Drain the spinach well and pat off any excess water with paper towels.

3 Fry the onion slowly in the oil for 5 minutes until softened. Add the spinach and continue to fry until just wilted. Drain off any excess liquid produced. Place on the pizza and sprinkle over the nutmeg.

4 Remove the shells from the eggs and slice. Arrange on the spinach.

5 Mix together the bread crumbs, cheese, and almonds, and sprinkle over. Drizzle with a little olive oil and season well.

6 Bake in a preheated oven for 18–20 minutes or until the edge is crisp and golden. Serve immediately.

SPINACH

If fresh spinach is unavailable, use frozen whole leaf spinach. Spinach carries a lot of water so drain out as much as possible or you will end up with a soggy base.

STEP 1

STEP 2

STEP 3

STEP 6

RATATOUILLE & LENTIL

The ultimate vegetarian pizza! Ratatouille and lentils on a whole wheat bread base are topped with vegetarian Cheddar and sunflower seeds. You can use canned green lentils, which do not have to be soaked or cooked before being used; you will need about ½ cup.

SERVES 2–4
OVEN: 400°F

2 oz green lentils
½ small eggplant, diced
1 small onion, sliced
1 garlic clove, crushed
3 tbsp olive oil
½ zucchini, sliced
½ red bell pepper, sliced
½ green bell pepper, sliced
7 oz can chopped tomatoes
1 tbsp chopped fresh oregano or 1 tsp dried
1 quantity Bread Dough Base made with
   whole wheat flour (see page 136)
2 oz vegetarian Cheddar cheese,
   sliced thinly
1 tbsp sunflower seeds
olive oil for drizzling
salt and pepper

1 Soak the lentils in hot water for 30 minutes. Drain and rinse; then simmer in a pan covered with fresh water for 10 minutes.

2 Sprinkle the eggplant with a little salt in a colander and allow the bitter juices to drain over a sink for about 20 minutes. Rinse and pat dry with paper towels.

3 Fry the onion and garlic slowly in the oil for 3 minutes. Add the zucchini, bell peppers, and eggplant. Cover and leave to "sweat" over a low heat for about 5 minutes.

4 Add the tomatoes, drained lentils, oregano, 2 tablespoons water, and seasoning. Cover and simmer for 15 minutes, stirring occasionally, adding more water if necessary.

5 Roll out or press the dough, using a rolling pin or your hands, into a 10 in. round on a lightly floured counter. Place on a large greased cookie sheet or pizza pan and push up the edge slightly. Cover and let rise slightly for 10 minutes in a warm place.

6 Spread the ratatouille over the dough base almost to the edge. Arrange the cheese slices on top and sprinkle over the sunflower seeds. Drizzle with a little olive oil and season.

7 Bake in a preheated oven for 18–20 minutes or until the edge is crisp and golden. Serve immediately.

THREE CHEESE & ARTICHOKE

Sliced artichokes combined with soft blue cheese, Cheddar, and Parmesan cheeses give a really delicious topping to this pizza. Artichoke hearts can be bought either canned or in jars in olive oil. If you use the ones in oil, you can use the oil to drizzle over the pizza before baking.

STEP 1

STEP 3

STEP 4

STEP 6

SERVES 2–4
OVEN: 400°F

1 quantity Bread Dough Base
  (see page 136)
1 quantity Special Tomato Sauce
  (see page 144)
2 oz soft blue cheese, sliced
4 oz artichoke hearts in oil, sliced
1/2 small red onion, chopped
1/3 cup grated Cheddar cheese
2 tbsp grated Parmesan cheese
1 tbsp chopped fresh thyme
oil from artichokes for drizzling
salt and pepper

1 Roll out or press the dough, using a rolling pin or your hands, into a 10 in. round on a lightly floured counter. Place the base on a large greased cookie sheet or pizza pan and push up the edge slightly.

2 Cover and leave to rise for 10 minutes in a warm place. Spread with the tomato sauce almost to the edge.

3 Arrange the soft blue cheese on the tomato sauce, followed by the artichoke hearts and red onion.

4 Mix the Cheddar and Parmesan together with the thyme and sprinkle the mixture over the pizza. Drizzle a little of the oil from the jar of artichokes over the pizza and season to taste.

5 Bake in a preheated oven for 18–20 minutes or until the edge is crisp and golden and the cheese is bubbling.

6 Serve immediately with a fresh salad of lettuce leaves and cherry tomato halves.

CHEESES AND SALADS

You can use any cheese of your choice, as long as it complements the others. Remember that a strongly flavored cheese will dominate the others. For the accompanying salad, buy a bag of mixed prepared lettuce leaves, as it saves buying several whole lettuces of different kinds.

STEP 1

STEP 2

STEP 3

STEP 4

GIARDINIERA

As the name implies, this colorful pizza should be topped with fresh vegetables grown in the garden, but as many of us do not have space to grow anything more than a few flowers, we have to rely on other sources. The vegetables used here are only a suggestion; you can replace them with the same quantity of anything that is available.

SERVES 2–4
OVEN: 400°F

6 fresh spinach leaves
1 quantity Potato Base (see page 140)
1 quantity Special Tomato Sauce
  (see page 144)
1 tomato, sliced
1 celery stick, sliced thinly
1/2 green bell pepper, cored, deseeded, and
  sliced thinly
1 baby zucchini, sliced
1/4 cup asparagus tips
1/4 cup whole kernel corn, defrosted if frozen
1/4 cup peas, defrosted if frozen
4 scallions, trimmed and chopped
1 tbsp chopped fresh mixed herbs, such as
  tarragon and parsley
1/2 cup grated Mozzarella cheese
2 tbsp grated Parmesan cheese
1 artichoke heart
olive oil for drizzling
salt and pepper

1 Remove any stalks from the spinach and wash the leaves in plenty of cold water. Pat dry with paper towels.

2 Roll out or press the potato base, using a rolling pin or your hands, into a large 10 in. round on a lightly floured counter. Place the round on a large greased cookie sheet or pizza pan and push up the edge a little to form a rim. Spread with the tomato sauce.

3 Arrange the spinach leaves on the sauce, followed by the tomato slices. Top with the remaining vegetables and herbs.

4 Mix together the cheeses and sprinkle over the pizza. Place the artichoke heart in the center. Drizzle the pizza with a little olive oil and season.

5 Bake in a preheated oven for 18–20 minutes or until the edges are crisp and golden. Serve immediately.

SPINACH

Bags of young spinach leaves are available in most supermarkets. The spinach has been washed and the large stalks have been removed. Use the required amounts of spinach on the pizza and use the remainder in a salad.

ROASTED VEGETABLE & GOAT CHEESE

Wonderfully colorful vegetables are roasted in olive oil with thyme and garlic. The goat cheese adds a nutty, piquant flavour.

STEP 1

STEP 2

STEP 3

STEP 5

SERVES 2–4
OVEN: 400°F

2 baby zucchini, halved lengthwise
2 baby eggplants, quartered lengthwise
1/2 red bell pepper, cored, deseeded, and cut
   into 4 strips
1/2 yellow bell pepper, cored, deseeded, and
   cut into 4 strips
1 small red onion, cut into wedges
2 whole garlic cloves
4 tbsp olive oil
1 tbsp red wine vinegar
1 tbsp chopped fresh thyme
1 quantity Bread Dough Base
   (see page 136)
1 quantity Tomato Sauce (see page 143)
3 oz goat cheese
salt and pepper
fresh basil leaves, to garnish

1 Place all the prepared vegetables in a large roasting pan. Mix together the olive oil, vinegar, thyme, and plenty of seasoning and pour over, coating all the vegetables well.

2 Bake in a preheated oven for 15–20 minutes until the skins on the vegetables have started to blacken in places. Turn the vegetables over half-way through the cooking process. Let the vegetables sit for 5 minutes after roasting.

3 Peel the roast bell peppers and the garlic cloves. Slice the garlic.

4 Roll out or press the dough, using a rolling pin or your hands, into a 10 in. round on a lightly floured counter. Place on a large greased cookie sheet or pizza pan and raise the edge a little. Cover and leave for 10 minutes to rise slightly in a warm place. Spread with the tomato sauce almost to the edge.

5 Arrange the roasted vegetables on top and dot with the cheese. Drizzle the oil and juices from the roasting pan over the pizza and season.

6 Bake in a preheated oven for 18–20 minutes or until the edge is crisp and golden. Serve immediately, garnished with basil leaves.

CHAPTER THIRTEEN

Different Pizza Shapes

We usually think of a pizza as being round, but pizzas can be made in many shapes and sizes. Often they are made in a rectangle and cut into squares or strips to serve.

If you use alternative bases to the more traditional doughs, you will get a variety of different shapes depending on what you use. For instance, Italian bread pizzas are long, as the bases are made from an Italian loaf that has been halved lengthwise. These make very good pizza bases, particularly as they are quick to prepare, and make perfect individual meals.

Pocket breads, English muffins, bread rolls, and croissants can all be used for bases. As they have all been pre-baked, care must be taken not to overbake them, as this will result in a dried-out base. In some cases it might be preferable to cook the pizza under a broiler rather than in the oven, as this would cook the topping without drying out the base.

Opposite: The Spanish Steps in the city of Rome, covered as always with a stunning floral display.

STEP 1

STEP 2

STEP 3

STEP 4

PISSALADIERE

This is a traditional Mediterranean-style pizza, in which the main ingredient is onions. A lattice pattern is made with anchovies and black olives. This pizza is rectangular in shape and can be cut into squares or strips to serve.

MAKES 6 SQUARES
OVEN: 400°F

4 tbsp olive oil
3 onions, sliced thinly
1 garlic clove, crushed
1 tsp soft brown sugar
1/2 tsp crushed fresh rosemary
7 oz can chopped tomatoes
1 quantity Bread Dough Base
 (see page 136)
2 tbsp grated Parmesan cheese
2 oz can anchovies
12–14 black olives
salt and black pepper

1 Heat 3 tablespoons of the oil in a large saucepan and add the onions, garlic, sugar, and rosemary. Cover and fry gently for 10 minutes until the onions have softened but not browned, stirring occasionally. Add the tomatoes, stir, and season well. Leave to cool slightly.

2 Roll out or press the dough, using a rolling pin or your hands, on a lightly floured counter to fit a 12 × 7 in. greased jelly roll pan. Place in the pan and push up the edges slightly.

3 Brush the remaining oil over the dough and sprinkle with the

cheese. Cover and let rise slightly in a warm place for about 10 minutes.

4 Spread the onion and tomato topping over the base. Remove the anchovies from the can, reserving the oil. Split each anchovy in half lengthwise and arrange on the pizza in a lattice pattern. Place olives in between the anchovies and drizzle over a little of the reserved oil. Season.

5 Bake in a preheated oven for 18–20 minutes or until the edges are crisp and golden. Cut into squares and serve immediately.

PARTY PIZZA

For a great party pizza, make twice the size in a large greased roasting pan, doubling up on the ingredients, and bake until the edges are golden.

STEP 1

STEP 2

STEP 3

STEP 5

HAWAIIAN MUFFINS

Halved toasted English muffins are topped with pineapple and prosciutto, which is an Italian dry-cured ham. Plain, whole wheat, or cheese muffins all make great pizza bases.

SERVES 4
OVEN: 400°F

4 English muffins
1 quantity Tomato Sauce (see page 143)
2 sun-dried tomatoes in oil, drained and
    chopped
2 oz prosciutto
2 rings canned pineapple, chopped
$^{1}/_{2}$ green bell pepper, cored, deseeded,
    and chopped
4 oz thinly sliced Mozzarella cheese
olive oil for drizzling
salt and pepper
small fresh basil leaves, to garnish

1 Cut the muffins in half and toast the cut side lightly.

2 Divide the sauce evenly between the muffins and spread over.

3 Sprinkle over the sun-dried tomatoes.

4 Cut the ham into thin strips and place on the muffins with the pineapple and green bell pepper.

5 Lay the Mozzarella slices on top of the pineapple and bell pepper.

6 Drizzle a little olive oil over the whole pizza and season.

7 Place under a preheated medium broiler and cook until the cheese melts and bubbles.

8 Serve immediately, garnished with small basil leaves.

MUFFINS

Muffins freeze well, so always keep some in the freezer for an instant pizza. To freeze muffins, put them into a plastic bag, seal, and label the bag with the date and contents.

PREPARING PINEAPPLE

To prepare a fresh pineapple, slice off the skin from the top, bottom, and sides. Remove the eyes with a sharp knife or the end of a potato peeler. Cut the pineapple into chunks. The pineapple will lose a lot of juice as you peel it – save as much as you can, and drink it later.

FRENCH BREAD PIZZAS

Halved French breads are a ready-made pizza base. The colors of the tomatoes and cheese contrast beautifully on top. Try an onion or a Granary bread, or Italian ciabatta bread, which makes a really good base.

STEP 2

SERVES 4
OVEN: 400°F

2 French Breads
1 quantity Tomato Sauce (see page 143)
4 plum tomatoes, sliced thinly lengthwise
5 oz thinly sliced Mozzarella cheese
10 black olives, cut into rings
8 fresh basil leaves, shredded
olive oil for drizzling
salt and pepper

1 Cut the French breads in half lengthwise and toast the cut side of the bread lightly.

2 Spread the toasted breads with the tomato sauce.

3 Arrange the tomato and Mozzarella slices alternately along the length.

4 Top with the olive rings and half the basil. Drizzle over a little olive oil and season well.

5 Either place under a preheated medium broiler and cook until the cheese melts and is bubbling or bake in a preheated oven for 15–20 minutes.

6 Sprinkle over the remaining basil and serve immediately.

STEP 3

DIFFERENT BREAD BASES

There are many different types of bread available which would be suitable for these pizzas. Italian ciabatta bread is made with olive oil and is available both plain and with different ingredients, such as small pieces of black olives or sun-dried tomatoes, mixed in.

INSTANT PIZZA

Make up double quantities and freeze half of the pizzas. Reheat them from frozen in the oven for about 15 minutes for an instant snack.

STEP 4

STEP 6

STEP 2

STEP 3

STEP 4

STEP 5

CALZONE

A calzone is like a pizza in reverse – it resembles a large turnover with the dough on the outside and the filling on the inside. In Italian the word "calzone" actually means pants! If you are going on a picnic, take a calzone pizza as it can be eaten cold and is easy to transport.

SERVES 2–4
OVEN: 400°F

1 quantity Bread Dough Base
  (see page 136)
1 egg, beaten
1 tomato
1 tbsp tomato paste
1 oz Italian salami, chopped
1 oz mortadella ham, chopped
1 oz Ricotta cheese
2 scallions, trimmed and chopped
¼ tsp dried oregano
salt and pepper

1 Roll out the dough into a 9 in. round on a lightly floured counter.

2 Brush the edge of the dough with a little beaten egg.

3 To skin the tomato, cut a cross in the skin and immerse it in boiling water for 45 seconds. Remove and rinse in cold water; the skin should slide off easily. Chop the tomato.

4 Spread the tomato paste evenly over the half of the round which is nearest to you. Scatter the salami, mortadella, and chopped tomato on top, then dot with the Ricotta and finally sprinkle over the scallions and oregano. Season well.

5 Fold the other half of the dough towards you to form a half moon. Press the edges together well to prevent the filling from coming out.

6 Place on a cookie sheet and brush with beaten egg to glaze. Make a hole in the top to allow steam to escape.

7 Bake in a preheated oven for 20 minutes or until golden.

VEGETARIAN VERSION

For a vegetarian calzone, replace the salami and mortadella with mushrooms or cooked chopped spinach.

STEP 1

STEP 4

STEP 6

STEP 7

CALIFORNIAN PEPPER

The vibrant colors of the bell peppers and onion make this a delightful pizza. Served cut into fingers, it is ideal for a party or buffet.

MAKES 8
OVEN: 400°F

1 quantity Bread Dough Base
  (see page 136)
2 tbsp olive oil
$^1/_2$ each red, green, and yellow bell pepper,
  cored, deseeded, and sliced thinly
1 small red onion, sliced thinly
1 garlic clove, crushed
1 quantity Tomato Sauce (see page 143)
3 tbsp raisins
$^1/_4$ cup pine nuts
1 tbsp chopped fresh thyme
olive oil for drizzling
salt and pepper

1 Roll out or press the dough, using a rolling pin or your hands, on a lightly floured counter to fit a 12×7 in. greased jelly roll pan.

2 Place in the pan and push up the edges slightly.

3 Cover and let rise slightly in a warm place for about 10 minutes.

4 Heat the oil in a large skillet. Add the bell peppers, onion, and garlic and fry gently for 5 minutes until they have softened but not browned. Leave to cool.

5 Spread the tomato sauce over the base almost to the edge.

6 Sprinkle over the raisins and top with the cooled bell pepper mixture. Add the pine nuts and thyme. Drizzle with a little olive oil and season well.

7 Bake in a preheated oven for 18–20 minutes or until the edges are crisp and golden. Cut into fingers and serve immediately.

RAISINS

Soak the raisins in some warm water for 15 minutes before adding them to the pizza, as this will keep them plump and moist when they are baked.

CHAPTER FOURTEEN

Inventive Pizzas

In this chapter anything goes! Pizzas can be topped with almost any ingredient, so let your imagination go and make up your own individual recipes.

Pizza-making can be really fun for children. Let them create animal or funny faces from a range of ingredients such as vegetables, cheese, and pasta. The results may help to encourage difficult eaters to clear their plates.

The Sunday brunch will never be the same again after trying a breakfast pizza. Experiment with different flavors and you will be surprised by what you can come up with.

Opposite: *Rome's famous Trevi Fountain.*

STEP 1

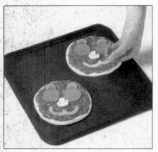

STEP 4

STEP 6

STEP 7

FUNNY FACES

These individual pizzas have faces made from sliced vegetables and spaghetti or noodles. Children love pizzas and will enjoy making their own. Use whatever suitable vegetables you have and let them have fun making all sorts of funny faces.

SERVES 4
OVEN: 400°F

1 quantity Bread Dough Base
  (see page 136)
1 oz spaghetti or egg noodles
1 quantity Tomato Sauce (see page 143)
8 slices pepperoni-style sausage
8 thin stalks celery
4 slices button mushrooms
4 slices yellow bell pepper
4 slices Mozzarella cheese
4 slices zucchini
olive oil for drizzling
8 peas

1 Divide the dough into 4 pieces. Roll each piece out into a 5 in. circle and place on greased cookie sheets. Cover and let rise slightly in a warm place for about 10 minutes.

2 Cook the spaghetti or egg noodles according to the instructions printed on the packet.

3 Divide the tomato sauce evenly between each pizza base and spread out almost to the edge.

4 To make the faces, use pepperoni slices for the main part of the eyes,

celery for the eyebrows, mushrooms for the noses, and bell pepper slices for the mouths.

5 Cut the Mozzarella and zucchini slices in half. Use the cheese for the cheeks and the zucchini for the ears.

6 Drizzle a little olive oil over each pizza and bake in a preheated oven for 12–15 minutes until the edges are crisp and golden.

7 Transfer the pizzas to serving plates and place the peas in the center of the eyes. Drain the spaghetti or noodles and arrange around the tops of the pizzas for hair. Serve immediately.

CAT PIZZA

Make cat-face pizzas by using endive for the ears, a mushroom for the nose, and spaghetti for whiskers. Cut out cat-eye shapes from pepperoni or bell peppers, and add a pasta bow tie.

STEP 2

STEP 3

STEP 4

STEP 6

BREAKFAST

For a really substantial start to the morning, try a breakfast pizza! Sausages, bacon, and mushrooms on a bread base topped with a fried egg will probably see you through the day.

SERVES 4
OVEN: 400°F

1 quantity Bread Dough Base
  (see page 136)
12 skinless cocktail sausages
3 tbsp oil
1 quantity Tomato Sauce (see page 143)
5 oz can baked beans
4 slices bacon
²/₃ cup baby button mushrooms, wiped
  and quartered
1 small tomato, cut into 8 wedges
¹/₄ cup Cheddar cheese, grated
4 eggs
salt and pepper

1 Roll out or press the dough, using a rolling pin or your hands, into a 10 in. round on a lightly floured counter. Place on a large greased cookie sheet or pizza pan and push up the edge slightly to form a rim. Cover and let rise slightly for 10 minutes in a warm place.

2 Brown the cocktail sausages in a skillet with 1 tablespoon of the oil.

3 Mix the tomato sauce with the baked beans and spread over the base almost to the edge. Add the sausages on top.

4 Cut the bacon into strips and arrange on the pizza with the mushrooms and tomato. Sprinkle over the cheese and season.

5 Bake in a preheated oven for 18–20 minutes or until the edge is crisp and golden.

6 Add the remaining oil to the skillet and fry the eggs. When the pizza is cooked, cut into 4 pieces and top each with a fried egg. Serve immediately.

PLANNING AHEAD

To save time in the morning, you can make the tomato sauce and bread dough the night before. After the dough has been kneaded, wrap well and place in the refrigerator (if it is cold enough, this should prevent the dough from rising). After rolling out, the dough will take about 10 minutes longer to rise.

SPICY MEATBALL

Small ground beef meatballs, spiced with chilies and cumin seeds and covered in cheese and bacon, are baked on a biscuit base.

STEP 1

SERVES 2–4
OVEN: 400°F

8 oz lean ground beef
1 oz chopped jalapeño chilies in brine
1 tsp cumin seeds
1 tbsp chopped fresh flat-leaf parsley
1 tbsp beaten egg
3 tbsp olive oil
1 quantity Biscuit Base (see page 138)
1 quantity Tomato Sauce (see page 143)
¼ cup sliced pimiento
2 slices bacon, cut into strips
½ cup grated Cheddar cheese
olive oil for drizzling
salt and pepper
chopped fresh flat-leaf parsley, to garnish

1 Mix the beef, chilies, cumin seeds, parsley, and egg together in a bowl and season. Form into 12 small meatballs. Cover and chill for 1 hour.

2 Heat the oil in a large skillet. Add the meatballs and brown all over. Remove with a perforated spoon or fish slice and drain on paper towels.

3 Roll out or press the dough, using a rolling pin or your hands, into a 10 in. round on a lightly floured counter. Place on a greased cookie sheet or pizza pan and push up the edge slightly to form a rim.

STEP 2

4 Spread with the tomato sauce almost to the edge. Arrange the meatballs on the pizza with the pimiento and bacon. Sprinkle over the cheese and drizzle with a little olive oil. Season.

5 Bake in a preheated oven for 18–20 minutes or until the edge is golden and crisp.

6 Serve immediately garnished with chopped parsley.

STEP 3

MEATBALLS

If possible, make the meatballs in time to chill them for an hour before frying as this will help to stop them from breaking up during cooking.

STEP 4

STEP 1

STEP 3

STEP 5

STEP 8

AVOCADO & HAM

A smoked ham and avocado salad is served on a pizza with a base enriched with chopped sun-dried tomatoes and black olives, which are kneaded into the dough.

SERVES 2–4
OVEN: 400°F

1 quantity Bread Dough Base
(see page 136)
4 sun-dried tomatoes, chopped
¼ cup chopped black olives
1 quantity Special Tomato Sauce
(see page 144)
4 small endive leaves, shredded
4 small radicchio lettuce leaves, shredded
1 avocado, peeled, pitted, and sliced
2 oz wafer-thin smoked ham
2 oz soft blue cheese, cut into small pieces
olive oil for drizzling
salt and pepper
chopped fresh chervil, to garnish

1 Knead the dough gently, adding the sun-dried tomatoes and olives until mixed in.

2 Roll out or press the dough, using a rolling pin or your hands, into a 10 in. round on a lightly floured counter. Place on a greased cookie sheet or pizza pan and push up the edge a little to form a rim.

3 Cover and let rise in a warm place for 10 minutes before spreading with tomato sauce almost to the edge.

4 Top the pizza with shredded endive and lettuce leaves and avocado slices.

5 Scrunch up the ham and add with the cheese.

6 Drizzle with a little olive oil and season well.

7 Bake in a preheated oven for 18–20 minutes or until the edge is crisp and golden.

8 Sprinkle with chervil to garnish and serve immediately.

HELPFUL HINTS

Before you use them, toss the avocado slices in a little fresh lemon juice to prevent the flesh from turning too brown. For a change, you could use wafer-thin smoked turkey instead of ham.

STEP-BY-STEP

ITALIAN
Cuisine

ITALIAN CUISINE

ITALIAN COOKING

Tourists flock in their millions to Italy, drawn by the ancient Roman architecture, the wealth of art galleries and churches, the Renaissance paintings, and the famous, and now carefully restored, frescos by Michelangelo on the ceiling and walls of the Sistine Chapel in the Vatican, Rome. They also go to enjoy the warm, friendly atmosphere and the food!

A culinary history

The Italian cuisine that we know today is the result of a very chequered history. In the past, many different races invaded the Italian peninsula. The Etruscans brought polenta and the Greeks introduced wonderful seafood cookery. The Romans not only developed the Greek style of cookery but wrote down their recipes – and they still exist today.

Many peoples passed through Italy and brought in new ideas. In 1861, the Unification of Italy brought 20 separate regions together under one flag, but the different styles of cooking remained unchanged.

ITALIAN FOOD REGION BY REGION

There are two main culinary zones in Italy: the wine and olive zone, which lies around Umbria, Liguria, and the South; and the cattle country, where the olive tree will not flourish – Emilia-Romagna, Lombardy, and Veneto – but where milk and butter are widely produced. Tuscany, however, uses both butter and oil in its cooking because both cattle and olive trees flourish in the area.

Piedmont

The name means "at the foot of the mountain", which it is, bordering on both France and Switzerland. Its fertile arable fields are irrigated by the many canals which flow through the region.

The food is substantial, peasant-type fare, though the fragrant white truffle is found in this region. Truffles can be finely flaked or grated and added to many of the smarter dishes, but they are wildly expensive. There is an abundance of wild mushrooms throughout the region. Garlic features strongly in the recipes and polenta, gnocchi, and rice are eaten in larger quantities than pasta, the former being offered as a first course when soup is not served. A large variety of game is also widely available.

Lombardy

The mention of the capital, Milan, produces immediate thoughts of the wonderful risotto named after the city and also the Milanese soufflé flavored strongly with lemon. Veal dishes,

including *vitello tonnato* and *osso buco*, are specialties of the region and other excellent meat dishes, particularly pot roasts, feature widely.

The lakes of the area produce a wealth of fresh fish. Rice and polenta are again popular but pasta also appears in many guises. The famous sweet yeasted cake Panettone is a product of this region.

Trentino-Alto Adige

This is an area with a strong German influence, particularly when it comes to the wines. There are also several German-style liqueurs produced, such as Aquavit, Kümmel, and Slivovitz.

The foods are robust and basic in this mountainous area with rich green valleys and lakes where fish are plentiful. In the Trentino area particularly, pasta and simple meat and variety meat dishes are popular, while in the Adige soups and pot roasts are favoured, often with added dumplings and spiced sausages.

Veneto

The cooking in this north-east corner is straightforward, with generous servings of polenta with almost everything. The land is intensively farmed, providing mostly cereals and wine. Pasta is less in evidence, with polenta, gnocchi, and rice more favoured. Fish, particularly shellfish, is in abundance and especially good seafood salads are widely available. There are also excellent robust soups and risottos flavored with the seafood and sausages of the area.

Liguria

The Genoese are excellent cooks, and all along the Italian Riviera can be found excellent trattoria which produce amazing fish dishes flavored with the local olive oil. Pesto sauce flavored with basil, cheese, and pine nuts comes from this area, along with other excellent sauces. The aroma of fresh herbs abounds, widely used in many dishes, including the famous pizzas.

Emilia-Romagna

This is a special region of high gastronomic importance, with an abundance of everything, and rich food is widely served. Tortellini and lasagne feature widely, along with many other pasta dishes, as do saltimbocca and other veal dishes. Parma is famous for its ham, *prosciutto di Parma*, thought to be the best in the world. Balsamic vinegar, which has grown in popularity over the past decade, is also produced here, from wine which is distilled until it is dark brown and extremely strongly flavored.

Tuscany

The Tuscans share a great pride in cooking and eating with the Emilians, and are known to have hefty appetites. Tuscany has everything: an excellent coastal area providing splendid fish, hills covered in vineyards, and fertile plains where every conceivable vegetable and fruit happily grows. There is plenty of game in the region, providing many interesting recipes; tripe cooked in a thick tomato sauce is popular along with many liver recipes; beans in many guises appear frequently, as well as pot roasts, steaks, and full-bodied soups, all of which are well flavored.

Florence has a wide variety of specialties, while Siena boasts the famous candied fruit cake called Panforte di Siena.

Umbria/Marches

Inland Umbria is famous for its pork, and the character of the cuisine is marked by the use of the local fresh ingredients, including lamb, game, and fish from the lakes, but is not spectacular on the whole. Spit-roasting and broiling is popular, and the excellent local olive oil is used both in cooking and to pour over dishes before serving. Black truffles, olives, fruit, and herbs are plentiful and feature in many recipes. Eastwards to the Marches the wealth of fish from the coast adds even more to the variety and the food tends to be more on the elaborate side, with almost every restaurant noted for its excellent cuisine. First-class sausages and cured pork come from the Marches, particularly on the Umbrian border, and pasta features widely all over the region.

Lazio

Rome is the capital of both Lazio and Italy and thus has become a focal point for specialties from all over Italy. Food from this region tends to be fairly simple and quick to prepare, hence the many pasta dishes with delicious sauces, gnocchi in various forms, and plenty of dishes featuring lamb and veal (saltimbocca being just one), and variety meats, all with plenty of herbs and seasonings giving really robust flavors

The cooking of today

The most significant divide for Italy's cuisine is that between the industrial north and the poorer south. The north, with its fertile plains, its mountains, and lakes, produces good-quality wines and dairy foods. By contrast, the sunnier, rockier south has olive groves, eggplants, tomatoes, and herbs. However, the regions do have features in common: the ingredients are fresh, techniques are simple, recipes are traditional, and cooking, even in restaurants, is home-style.

BECHAMEL SAUCE

1¼ cups milk
2 bay leaves
3 cloves
1 small onion
¼ cup butter, plus extra for
    greasing
6 tbsp all-purpose flour
1¼ cups light cream
large pinch grated nutmeg
salt and pepper

1. Pour the milk into a small saucepan and add the bay leaves. Press the cloves into the onion, add to the pan, and bring the milk to a boil. Remove from the heat and set it aside to cool.

2. Strain the milk into a pitcher and rinse the saucepan. Melt the butter in the saucepan and stir in the flour. Stir for 1 minute, then gradually pour on the milk, stirring constantly. Cook the sauce for 3 minutes, then pour on the cream and bring it to a boil. Remove from the heat and season with nutmeg, salt, and pepper.

CHEESE SAUCE

2 tbsp butter
1 tbsp all-purpose flour
1 cup milk
2 tbsp light cream
pinch grated nutmeg
1½ oz Cheddar cheese, grated
1 tbsp grated Parmesan cheese

1. Melt the butter in a saucepan, stir in the flour and cook for 1 minute.

and delicious sauces. Vegetables feature along with the fantastic fruits which are always in abundance in the local markets; and beans appear both in soups and many other dishes. The main theme of this region is strongly flavored food with robust sauces.

Abruzzi and Molise

Formerly counted as just one region called Abruzzi e Molise, these regions have an interior of mountains with river valleys, high plateaux, densely forested areas, and a coastal plain. The cuisine here is deeply traditional, with local hams and cheeses from the mountain areas, interesting sausages with plenty of garlic and other seasonings, cured meats, and wonderful fish and seafood, which is the main produce of the coastal areas, where fishing boats abound on the beaches. Lamb features widely: tender, juicy, and well-flavored with herbs.

Campania

Naples is the home of pasta dishes, served with a splendid tomato sauce (with many variations) famous worldwide. Pizza is said to have been created in Naples and now has spread to the north of the country and indeed all over the world.

Fish abounds, with *fritto misto* and *fritto pesce* being great favorites, varying daily depending on the catch. Fish stews are robust and varied and shellfish in particular is often served with pasta. Cutlets and steaks are excellent, served with strong sauces usually flavored with garlic, tomatoes, and herbs: pizzaiola steak is one of the favorites. Excellent Mozzarella cheese is produced locally and

used to create the crispy Mozzarella in Carozza, again served with a garlicky tomato sauce. Sweet dishes are popular too, often with flaky pastry and Ricotta cheese, and the seasonal fruit salads laced with wine or liqueur take a lot of beating.

Puglia (Apulia)

The ground is stony but it produces good fruit, olive groves, vegetables, and herbs, and, of course, there is a large amount of seafood from the sea. Puglians are said to be champion pasta eaters: many of the excellent pasta dishes are exclusive to the region both in shape and ingredients. Mushrooms abound and are always added to the local pizzas.

Oysters and mussels are plentiful, and so is octopus. Brindisi is famous for its shellfish – both the seafood salads and risottos are truly memorable. But it is not all fish or pasta: lamb is roasted and stewed to perfection and so is veal, always with plenty of herbs.

Basilicata

This is a sheep-farming area, mainly mountainous, where potent wines are produced to accompany a robust cuisine largely based on pasta, lamb, pork, game, and abundant dairy produce. The salamis and cured meats are excellent, as are the mountain hams. Lamb is flavored with the herbs and grasses on which it feeds. Wonderful thick soups – true minestrone – are produced in the mountains, and eels and fish are plentiful in the lakes. Chili peppers are grown in this region and appear in many of the recipes. They are not overpoweringly strong, although the flavors of the region in general tend to be quite strong and intense. The cheeses are excellent, good fruit is grown, and interesting local bread is baked in huge loaves.

Calabria

This is the toe of Italy, where orange and lemon groves flourish along with olive trees and a profusion of vegetables, especially eggplants which are cooked in a variety of ways.

Chicken, rabbit, and guinea fowl are often on the menu. Pizzas feature largely, often with a fishy topping. Mushrooms grow well in the Calabrian climate and feature in many dishes from sauces and stews to salads. Pasta comes with a great variety of sauces including baby artichokes, eggs, meat, cheese, mixed vegetables, the large sweet bell peppers of the region, and of course garlic. The fish is excellent too and fresh tuna and swordfish are available, along with many other varieties.

Like most southern Italians, the Calabrians are sweet-toothed and many desserts and cakes are flavored with aniseed, honey, and almonds and feature the plentiful figs of the region.

Sicily

This is the largest island in the Mediterranean and the cuisine is based mainly on fish and vegetables. Fish soups, stews, and salads appear in unlimited forms, including tuna, swordfish, mussels, and many more; citrus fruits are widely grown along with almonds and pistachio nuts, and the

local wines, including the dark, sweet, dessert wine Marsala, are excellent.

Meat is often given a long, slow cooking, or else is ground and shaped before cooking. Game is plentiful and is often cooked in sweet-sour sauces containing the local black olives.

Pasta abounds again with more unusual sauces as well as the old favorites. All Sicilians have a love of desserts, cakes, and especially ice-cream. Cassata and other ice-creams from Sicily are famous all over the world, and the huge variety of flavors of both cream ices and granita makes it difficult to decide which is your favorite.

Sardinia

A pretty island with a wealth of flowers in the spring, but the landscape dries out in the summer from the hot sun. The national dish is suckling pig or newborn lamb cooked on an open fire or spit, and rabbit, game, and variety meat dishes are also very popular.

The sweet dishes are numerous and often extremely delicate, and for non-sweet eaters there is fresh fruit of almost every kind in abundance.

Fish is top quality, with excellent sea bass, lobsters, tuna, mullet, eels, and mussels in good supply.

The island has a haunting aroma which drifts from many kitchens – it is myrtle (*mirto*), a local herb which is added to anything and everything from chicken to the local liqueur; and along with the wonderful cakes and breads of Sardinia, myrtle will long remain a memory of the island when you have returned home.

2. Gradually pour on the milk, stirring all the time. Stir in the cream and season the sauce with nutmeg, salt, and pepper.

3. Simmer the sauce for 5 minutes to reduce, then remove it from the heat and stir in the cheeses. Stir until the cheese has melted and blended into the sauce.

LAMB SAUCE

2 tbsp olive oil
1 large onion, sliced
2 celery stalks, thinly sliced
1 lb lean lamb, ground
3 tbsp tomato paste
5 oz bottled sun-dried tomatoes, drained and chopped
1 tsp dried oregano
1 tbsp red wine vinegar
²/₃ cup chicken stock
salt and pepper

1. Heat the oil in a skillet over a medium heat and fry the onion and celery until the onion is translucent. Add the lamb and fry, stirring frequently, until it browns.

2. Stir in the tomato paste, sun-dried tomatoes, oregano, vinegar, and stock. Season with salt and pepper.

3. Bring to a boil and cook, uncovered, for 20 minutes or until the meat has absorbed the stock. Taste and adjust the seasoning if necessary.

BASIC PASTA DOUGH

If you get caught up in the enthusiasm of pasta making, you might like to buy a machine to roll, stretch, and cut the dough. However, once it is fully and evenly stretched, it is surprisingly easy to cut by hand.

SERVES 4

1 cup all-purpose flour, plus extra
    for dusting
²/₃ cup fine semolina
1 tsp salt
2 tbsp olive oil
2 eggs
2–3 tbsp hot water

1. Strain the flour, semolina, and salt into a bowl and make a well in the center. Pour in half the oil and add the eggs. Add 1 tablespoon of hot water and, using your fingertips, work to a smooth dough. Sprinkle on a little more water if necessary to make the dough pliable.

2. Lightly dust a board with flour, turn the dough out, and knead it until it is elastic and silky. This might take 10–12 minutes. Dust the dough with more flour if your fingers become sticky.

3. Alternatively, put the eggs, 1 tablespoon hot water and the oil in the bowl of a food processor and process for a few seconds. Add the flour, semolina, and salt and process until smooth. Sprinkle on a

GETTING TO KNOW PASTA

Pasta means "paste" or "dough" in Italian, and many of the popular dishes have their origins in Italy, where it has been produced since the thirteenth century or earlier.

The principal ingredients of traditional pasta are modest, although today there are more types of fresh and dried pasta available. By far the most popular type is made from durum wheat, which is milled to form fine semolina grains and then extruded through drums fitted with specially perforated discs, producing an estimated 600 different pasta varieties.

Varieties of pasta

Pasta is made from either the endosperm of the wheat, or from the whole wheat, which contains more dietary fiber. Other basic types are made from ground buckwheat, which gives the product a greyish color and nutty flavor that combines well with vegetable and herb sauces; with the addition of spinach paste, which produces an attractive green color – *lasagne verde* is a popular example; and with a proportion of tomato paste, which produces a deep coral coloring. *Pasta all'uovo*, made with eggs, is produced in a range of flat shapes, fresh or dried.

As well as green and red pasta, there are other colors available: saffron pasta is an attractive yellow-orange color, beetroot-hued pasta is a deep pink, and pasta colored with squid ink is a dramatic black which makes any dish truly eye-catching. You can also buy or make pasta flecked with chopped basil and other herbs.

Aside from these refinements of color and flavor, pasta is generally divided into three main categories: long and folded pasta, noodles, and short pasta.

Since dried pasta has a shelf life of up to 6 months (see page 200) and fresh pasta may be frozen for up to 6 months, it is a good idea to build up your own selection of varieties with which to surprise your family and friends.

Pasta dictionary

The following is a glossary of some of the most popular pasta shapes.

anelli and anellini small rings for soups

bozzoli deeply-ridged, cocoon-like shapes

bucatini long, medium-thick tubes

cappelletti wide-brimmed hat shapes

cappelli d'angelo "angel's hair", thinner than cappellini

cappellini fine strands of ribbon pasta

casareccia short curled lengths of pasta twisted at one end

cavatappi short, thick corkscrew shapes

conchiglie ridged shells

conchigliette little shells used in soup

cornetti ridged shells

cresti di gallo curved shapes

ditali, ditalini short tubes

eliche loose spiral shapes

elicoidali short, ridged tubes

farfalle bows

fedeli, fedelini fine tubes twisted into "skeins"

festonati short lengths, like garlands

fettuccine ribbon pasta, narrower than tagliatelle

fiochette, fiochelli small bow shapes

frezine broad, flat ribbons

fusilli spindles, or short spirals

fusilli bucati thin spirals, like springs

gemelli "twins", two pieces wrapped together

gramigna meaning "grass" or "weed"; the shapes look like sprouting seeds

lasagne flat, rectangular sheets

linguini long, flat ribbons

lumache smooth, snail-like shells popular with seafood sauces

lumachine U-shaped flat noodles

macaroni, maccheroni long or short-cut tubes, may be ridged or elbow-shaped

maltagliati triangular-shaped pieces, traditionally used in bean soups

noodles fine, medium or broad flat ribbons

orecchiette dished ear shapes

orzi tiny pasta, like grains of rice, used in soups

pappardelle widest ribbons, either straight or sawtooth-edged

pearlini tiny discs

penne short, thick tubes with diagonal-cut ends

pipe rigate ridged, curved pipe shapes

rigatoni thick, ridged tubes

ruoti wheels

semini seed shapes

spaghetti fine, medium, or thick rods

spirale two rods twisted into spirals

strozzapreti "priest strangler", double twisted strands

tagliarini flat ribbon, thinner than tagliatelle

tagliatelle broad, flat ribbons

tortiglione thin, twisted tubes

vermicelli fine, slender strands usually sold folded into "skeins"

ziti tagliati short, thick tubes

Nutritional value

Pasta has frequently had to answer to the charge that it is a fattening food which must be avoided by anyone who is on a weight-reducing diet. The answer to that charge is that it may not be the pasta that piles on the calories, but more likely some of the sauces we choose to serve with it.

This table shows you some of the dietary and nutritional credentials of dry pasta.

per 4 oz

Average moisture content	11.10
Protein	13.20
Fat	2.80
Dietary fiber (approx.)	10.00
Starch (as monosaccharide)	65.70
Calories	327.00

little more hot water if necessary to make the dough pliable. Transfer to an electric mixer and knead using the dough hook for 2–3 minutes.

4. Divide the dough into 2 equal pieces. Cover a counter with a clean cloth or dish cloth and dust it liberally with flour. Place one portion of the dough on the floured cloth and roll it out as thinly and evenly as possible, stretching the dough gently until the pattern of the weave shows through. Cover it with a cloth and roll out the second piece in a similar way.

5. Use a ruler and a sharp knife blade to cut long, thin strips for noodles, or small confectionery cutters to cut rounds, stars, or other decorative shapes.

6. Cover the dough shapes with a clean cloth and leave them in a cool place (not the refrigerator) for 30–45 minutes to become partly dry, or place them in an airtight container for up to 24 hours.

7. Cook the fresh pasta in a large pan of boiling salted water, adding 1 tablespoon olive oil, for 3–4 minutes, until almost tender. Drain the pasta in a colander and serve with the sauce of your choice.

SPINACH & RICOTTA RAVIOLI

SERVES 4

*1 recipe basic pasta dough
(see pages 198–9)
12 oz frozen spinach, thawed
and chopped
¾ cup Ricotta cheese, or 3 oz each
full-fat soft cheese and cottage
cheese
4 tbsp grated Parmesan
salt and pepper
large pinch grated nutmeg*

*FOR THE SAUCE
2 tbsp butter
⅔ cup crème fraîche
grated nutmeg*

1. Turn the chopped spinach into a colander and use a wooden spoon to press out as much of the liquid as possible.

2. Mix together the spinach and cheeses and season the mixture with salt, pepper, and nutmeg. (For a smooth filling, you can mix the ingredients in a food processor.)

3. Divide the dough into 2 equal pieces and roll out each one as described on page 199. Cut one sheet into strips about 3 in. wide. Place small heaps of the filling at 3 in. intervals close to one side of each strip. Fold the strips over, press the edges to seal them and repeat with the remainder of the dough. Cut out the ravioli squares. A pastry wheel is useful for this, as it helps to seal the joins as it cuts.

COOKING PASTA

The real enjoyment of pasta depends upon the cooking; undercooked, and it will be unyielding and taste of raw flour; overcooked, and it will be soft and stick. The Italians describe the perfect texture as *al dente*, meaning that the pasta is still slightly resistant to the bite.

Cooking times vary according to the type and volume of the pasta, and you should always follow those recommended on the packet. In general, fresh pasta will be cooked in 3–5 minutes, dried pasta in around 6 minutes for fine strands such as vermicelli; 7–12 minutes for quick-cooking macaroni, spaghetti and noodles; and 10–15 minutes for cannelloni tubes and sheets of lasagne.

Whatever the pasta type, have ready a pan of water at a steady, rolling boil. Add salt, and 1 tablespoon of olive oil, to prevent sticking. Add the pasta gradually, a handful or a few strands at a time so that the water continues to boil and the pasta is kept separate. Do not completely cover the pan, or the water will boil over. Leave it uncovered, or partly covered. Drain the cooked pasta into a colander and, if it is not to be served at once, return it to the pan with a little olive oil.

How much to allow

It is not possible to say exactly how much pasta to allow for each person. It is worth remembering that dried pasta more than doubles in volume during cooking, absorbing water until it is rehydrated. The usual practice is to allow 1–2 oz dried pasta per person for a first course or a salad, and 3–4 oz dried pasta for a main dish.

Storing freezing pasta

Dried pasta will keep in good condition for up to six months. Keep it in the package, and reseal it once you have opened it, or transfer the pasta to an airtight jar.

Fresh pasta has a very short storage life, only one or two days in the refrigerator, so buy it only when you want to serve it.

Cooked pasta may be stored for up to three days in the refrigerator. If the pieces have stuck together, turn them in a colander and run warm water through them. Drain well, then toss the pasta in hot olive oil or melted butter before serving.

It is possible to freeze cooked pasta for up to 3 months. But it must be thawed at room temperature before reheating.

PASTA MACHINES

Pasta machines that will stretch and roll the dough are widely available. You will also need plenty of space for the rolled-out dough, as well as somewhere to hang the dough to dry.

The method is to feed the pasta through the rollers repeatedly, one notch thinner each time. This is time-consuming but important, as the pasta needs to keep its elasticity.

To roll the pasta from the recipe on page 198-9, first divide the dough into 2 pieces. If the pasta strip becomes too long and unwieldy as it stretches, cut it again. Roll until all the pieces have gone through the machine at each setting. Lay the pasta out on dish cloths to dry until it feels leathery which is when it is ready to be cut. The machine will cut pasta into strips for ribbon pasta; other shapes will have to be cut by hand. To use the pasta strips immediately, place a dish cloth over the back of a chair and hang the strips to dry.

PASTA SAUCES

Creative cooks will enjoy partnering their favorite sauces with a variety of pastas. Although there are classic combinations such as Spaghetti Bolognese and Spaghetti Carbonara, there are no rules, just guidelines, which are largely a matter of practicality, appearance, and taste. For example, use pasta shells to evoke the appropriate image and texture when eating with fish and shell-fish sauces.

Cheeses with pasta

Some cheeses have a natural affinity with pasta dishes and appear frequently in recipes.

Ricotta A milky white, soft, and crumbly Italian cheese which resembles cottage cheese. It is low in fat, being made from whey, but some varieties produced now have whole milk added. If you cannot obtain Ricotta, use another low-fat soft cheese. To obtain a smooth-textured sauce or filling press the substitute through a sieve.

Parmesan A mature and exceptionally hard cheese produced in Italy, Parmesan is the most important of flavorings for pasta. It may be useful to have a small carton of ready-grated Parmesan in the refrigerator, but you will find that it quickly loses its pungency and "bite". For that reason, it is better to buy small quantities of the cheese in one piece and grate it yourself. Tightly wrapped in

plastic wrap and foil, it can be kept in the refrigerator for several months. Grate it just before serving, for maximum flavor.

Pecorino A hard sheep's milk cheese which resembles Parmesan and is often used for grating over dishes. It has a sharp flavor and is only used in small quantities.

Mozzarella Another highly popular cheese, this is a soft cheese, with a piquant flavor, traditionally made from water buffalo's milk. Buffalo milk is now scarce, and so this cheese is often made with cow's milk. It can be used fresh, most popularly in salads, and also provides a tangy layer in baked dishes.

OLIVE OIL

Olive oil, which is at the heart of so many pasta dishes, has a personality all of its own, and each variety has its own characteristic flavor.

Extra-virgin olive oil This is the finest grade, made from the first, cold pressing of hand gathered olives. Always use extra-virgin oil for salad dressings.

Virgin olive oil This oil has a fine aroma and color, and is also made by cold pressing. It may have a slightly higher acidity level than extra-virgin oil.

Refined or "pure" olive oil This is made by treating the paste residue from the pressings with heat or solvents to remove the residual oil.

Olive oil is a blend of refined and virgin olive oil.

4. Cook the ravioli in a large pan of boiling water, to which you have added salt and 1 tablespoon olive oil, for 3–4 minutes.

5. Heat together the butter and crème fraîche and season with salt, pepper, and nutmeg.

6. Drain the pasta in a colander, turn it into a warmed serving dish, and pour over the sauce. Toss the ravioli to coat it thoroughly.

TOMATO SAUCE

2 tbsp olive oil
1 small onion, chopped
1 garlic clove, chopped
15 oz can chopped tomatoes
2 tbsp chopped parsley
1 tsp dried oregano
2 bay leaves
2 tbsp tomato paste
1 tsp sugar

1. To make the tomato sauce, heat the oil in a skillet over a medium heat and fry the onion until it is translucent. Add the garlic and fry for 1 further minute.

2. Stir in the chopped tomatoes, parsley, oregano, bay leaves, tomato paste and sugar and bring the sauce to the boil.

3. Simmer, uncovered, until the sauce has reduced by half, about 15–20 minutes. Taste the sauce and adjust the seasoning if necessary. Discard the bay leaves.

TIPS

Pizza bases and their ingredients

Buy compressed fresh yeast in bulk and freeze in $^1/_2$-oz quantities ready to use whenever needed.

To give the base extra flavor and a different texture, try adding to the flour fresh or dried herbs, chopped nuts, or seeds, such as poppy, sunflower, and sesame.

Always use a good olive oil such as extra virgin for the best flavor.

If time is short, place the bread dough in a food processor to knead for a few minutes.

If you have made the bread dough or biscuit base too wet, add a little extra flour and work it in. If the base is too dry, add a little extra water or milk in the same way.

Bread dough bases can be kept for several days before being used. After kneading, carefully wrap in plastic wrap to prevent them from drying out in the refrigerator. Allow extra time for the dough to rise, as it will take a while for the dough to warm up and for the yeast to begin to work.

If the dough is left uncovered and develops a crust, cover it with a damp cloth and the crust will soon disappear.

MAKING PIZZAS

The pizza has become a universally popular food, in every form from the genuine article – thin, crisp, and oven-baked – to frozen and fast-food pizza slices. The delightful aroma of freshly baked bread topped with tomatoes, fresh herbs, and cheese rarely fails to have a mouthwatering effect.

As well as being economical and popular, few other dishes are as versatile as the pizza, thanks to the countless possible permutations of bases and toppings that can be served to suit every palate and every occasion.

History of the pizza

Although there is much speculation about where pizza in its simplest form was first invented, it is usually associated with the old Italian city of Naples. It was then a simple street food, richly flavored and quickly made. It was not always round and flat as we know it today, but was originally folded up like a book, with the filling inside, and eaten by hand. Pizzas were usually sold on the streets by street criers who carried them around in copper cylindrical drums kept hot by coals from the pizza ovens.

The word "pizza" actually means any kind of pie. The classic Napoletana pizza is probably the best-known of the many varieties. This consists of a thin crust of dough topped simply with a fresh tomato sauce, Mozzarella cheese, olives, anchovies, and a sprinkling of oregano. When baked, the flavors blend perfectly together to give the distinctive aromatic pizza. Another classic is the "Margherita" pizza, named after the Italian Queen Margherita. Bored with their usual cuisine when on a visit to Naples, she asked to sample a local specialty. The local "Pizzaiolo" created a pizza in the colors of the Italian flag – red tomatoes, green basil, and white Mozzarella. The Queen was delighted, and it became widely celebrated.

BASIC PIZZA INGREDIENTS

Pizzas are made from very basic ingredients and are very simple to cook. Although making your own base and topping can be a little time-consuming, it is very straightforward, and you end up with a delicious home-baked dish, as well as a sense of achievement.

Flour

Traditional pizza bases are made from bread dough, which is usually made with strong bread flour. However, for the best results use ordinary all-purpose flour. A strong flour will make the dough very difficult to stretch into whatever shape you choose to make your pizza.

For a brown bread base, use one of the many types of whole wheat flours available on the market, such as stoneground whole wheat or wheat meal. Wheatgerm or bran can also be added to white flour for extra flavor, fiber, and interest. Or you could mix equal quantities of whole wheat and white flour.

Always sift the flour first, as this will remove any lumps and help to incorporate air into the flour, which will in turn help to produce a light dough. If you sift whole wheat flours, there will be some bran and other bits left in the strainer, which are normally tipped back so that their goodness and fiber are added to the sifted flour.

Yeast thrives in warm surroundings, so all the ingredients for the bread dough base should be warm, as should the equipment used. If the tepid yeast liquid is added to a cold bowl containing cold flour, it will quickly cool down. This will retard the growth of the yeast, and the dough will take much longer to rise. If the flour is kept in a cool closet or larder, remember to get it out in plenty of time to allow it to warm to room temperature before you use it. Sift the flour into a large mixing bowl, then place it somewhere warm, such as an airing closet or even in an oven on the lowest setting. Do not allow it to overheat, as this will kill the yeast.

Salt

Add the required amount of salt to the flour when sifting, as this will help to distribute it evenly throughout the resulting mixture. Salt is important, as it helps to develop the gluten in the flour. Gluten is the protein which produces the characteristic elasticity of the dough, but mostly it provides the dough with its flavor.

Yeast

There are three types of yeast available: compressed fresh, dried fresh, and easy-blend. Fresh yeast is usually found in health-food shops and is not expensive. Dissolve ½ oz fresh yeast in 3½ fl oz tepid water with ½ tsp sugar and allow it to froth before adding it to the flour – about 5 minutes. The frothiness indicates that

the yeast is working. Compressed fresh yeast will keep for 4 to 5 days in the refrigerator. Make sure it is well covered, as it will dry out very quickly.

Dried yeast can be found in envelopes or drums in most supermarkets and drug stores. It has a shelf life of about 6 months, so buy only a small drum if you are not going to make bread dough on a regular basis. It is easy to make up a dough that won't rise, only to find out too late that the yeast has passed the sell-by date. Like compressed yeast, add it to the tepid water with a little sugar, and stir to dissolve. Let the mixture sit for 10–15 minutes until froth develops on the surface.

Easy-blend yeast is the simplest to use, as it is simply stirred dry into the flour before the water is added. It is available in envelope form and can be found in most supermarkets.

Water

It has been said that Naples produces the best pizzas because of the quality of its water! But as that may be a bit far to travel just to make a pizza, your local water will have to suffice. The water must be tepid, as this is the optimum temperature for the yeast to grow. Take care to add just the right amount of water stated in the recipe. If you add too much water, the dough will be difficult to handle and the cooked base will be too hard.

Kneading

This can be the most daunting procedure in bread-making, but it is a very necessary one. The best way of doing it is

Fillings and toppings

Avoid using starchy topping ingredients, as the base is very substantial and you will end up with a heavy pizza.

Make sure that you season the tomato sauce well, as this is the basis of the pizza, and a bland sauce will make for a bland pizza. Using a bay leaf makes a considerable difference – but don't forget to take it out!

Do not overfill a pizza, as it will overflow in the oven and will be difficult to eat.

Make a rim around the edge of the dough, as this will help to keep the topping on.

When making pizza for several people with differing tastes, place different toppings on separate sections of the pizza, or make individual ones in a selection of flavors. They can all cook at the same time, making it easy to suit all tastes.

To make pizza easier to handle, put the heavier topping ingredients near the edge of the pizza rather than in the middle. This will help to prevent it from sagging at the point when cut into wedges.

Drain all the pizza ingredients as much as possible before they are used. If you use spinach, squeeze out as much water as possible, or you will end up with a soggy pizza.

Grease the pizza pan or cookie sheet well, to prevent the pizza from sticking.

Serving
Always serve a pizza as soon as it leaves the oven, as the cheese will set slightly and lose its elasticity as it cools down.

Place the pizza on a warmed serving plate when it comes out of the oven, to prevent it from going cold too quickly. Use a couple of large fish slices to transfer the pizza from the cookie sheet or pizza pan to the serving plate.

Pizzas make excellent party food. Make them in large rectangles and cut into squares to serve.

Leftovers
Any leftover Mozzarella cheese can be grated and frozen, ready for the next time you want to make a pizza.

Leftover tomato sauce can be used up by adding it to casseroles, soups, and pasta dish sauces such as spaghetti and lasagne.

Accompaniments
Follow a pizza meal with a refreshing dessert, such as fresh fruit salad, sorbet, or ice cream. Zabaglione, a light Italian dessert of eggs, sugar, and Marsala wine, makes a perfect ending.

to take the edge of the dough that is furthest away from you and pull it into the center towards you, then push it down with the heel of your hand, turning the dough round with your other hand as you go. The kneading process mixes all the ingredients together and strengthens the gluten, which holds the bubbles of air created by the yeast, which in turn causes the dough to rise. The dough must be kneaded for at least 5 minutes or until it becomes smooth and pliable and is no longer sticky.

Try adding extra ingredients to the dough when kneading, such as chopped sun-dried tomatoes or olives, to create a more interesting base.

The tomato sauce
Every pizza must have tomato sauce of some kind as the basis of the topping. This can be made using either canned or fresh tomatoes. There are many types of canned tomato available – for example, plum tomatoes, or tomatoes chopped in water, or chopped strained tomato (passata). The chopped variety are often canned with added flavors such as garlic, basil, onion, chili, and mixed herbs, which will add more interest to your sauce. Make sure the sauce is well seasoned before adding it to your base, as a tasteless sauce will spoil your pizza.

Cheese
The cheese most often associated with the pizza is, of course, Mozzarella. It is a mild, white, delicate cheese traditionally made from buffalo milk. The best feature of this cheese as far as pizzas are concerned is its ability to melt and

produce strings of cheese when a slice is cut and pulled away. It is sold in supermarkets, wrapped in small bags of whey to keep it moist. Slice, grate, or cut it into small pieces before placing it on the pizza. Many supermarkets stock bags of pre-grated Mozzarella cheese, which is a great timesaver.

The other cheeses most often found on pizzas are Parmesan and Cheddar. The recipes in this book use a variety of different cheeses. If you are using strongly flavored topping ingredients such as anchovies and olives, a milder-tasting cheese may be more suitable. Experiment with different cheeses to suit your taste.

TOPPING INGREDIENTS
There are a number of classic ingredients that are used regularly in pizza toppings, such as olives, anchovies, capers, mushrooms, bell peppers, artichokes, and chilies, but most ingredients are suitable, provided they are used in complementary combinations.

Be adventurous and experiment, but don't be afraid to stick to simple combinations of just two or three ingredients – often the simplest pizzas are the most delicious and the most memorable, as the flavors don't fight each other.

Herbs
Whenever possible, use fresh herbs. They are becoming more readily available, especially since the introduction of "growing" herbs, small pots of herbs which you buy from the supermarket or greengrocer and grow at home. This not

only ensures the herbs are as fresh as possible, but also provides a continuous supply.

If you use dried herbs, remember that you need only about one third of dried to fresh. The most popular pizza herbs are basil, oregano, and parsley, although you can experiment with your favorite ones. Torn leaves of fresh basil on a tomato base is a simple but deliciously aromatic combination.

Baking
Traditionally pizzas are cooked in special ovens on a stone hearth. A large peel or paddle is used to slide them in and out. But at home it is best to place the dough on a cookie sheet or in a pizza pan. The dough will expand while cooking, so make sure the cookie sheet is big enough. Always push up the edge of the dough to form a rim to prevent the topping from spilling over while it cooks.

Time-savers
Fortunately for the busy cook, pizzas are an easy food to package and chill or freeze, ready to be cooked on demand. There is a wide range of ready-made pizza bases. Some come in package form and only need to be mixed and shaped before they are ready for a topping, which can also be bought separately, most often in jars.

Pizzas are also sold complete with a variety of toppings, which you can bake as they are, or add more toppings yourself. Although they never seem to taste as good as a real homemade pizza, they can be very useful to keep on hand. Jars of peppers, sun-dried tomatoes, and

artichokes in olive oil make very good toppings, and will keep for quite a while in your larder.

Serving
Pizzas should be served as soon as they leave the oven. Cut the pizza into wedges or strips using a sharp knife or pizza cutter. As pizza slices are easy to eat by hand, they make great party food.

Crisp salads, coleslaw, and garlic bread go well with pizzas and help to make a balanced meal. Due to their rich flavor pizzas are best served with a well-chilled Italian table wine such as Frascati, Valpolicella or Chianti. If you are not a wine drinker, beer will go with pizza just as well.

Freezing
Pizzas are ideal standby food, as you can make and freeze them in advance, and both the bread dough and the complete pizza can be frozen. Make up double quantities of dough and freeze the half that is unused after it has been kneaded. Wrap in plastic wrap and place in a freezer bag. Defrost at room temperature and allow to rise as normal. Alternatively, rise and roll out the dough, top with tomato sauce, cheese, and any other topping ingredients and bake for only 10 minutes. Cool, wrap in a polythene bag, and place in the freezer. Cook straight from the freezer in a hot oven for about 15 minutes.

The tomato sauce will keep well in a screw-topped jar in the refrigerator for up to a week, or can be placed in freezer-proof containers and frozen if you need to keep it for longer periods.

Garlic bread
Garlic bread is often served with pizza. Mix 1–2 cloves of crushed garlic with 4 oz butter and spread it in between diagonal cuts made in a French bread stick. Wrap in foil and place in the bottom of the oven for 5 or 6 minutes while the pizza is cooking.

For herb bread, add chopped fresh parsley and chives to the butter before spreading it on the bread.

Salads
Salad-making has never been so simple, thanks to the bags of prepared salads available in most supermarkets. Choose a selection of unusual and exotic salad leaves to add color and crunch to your salad. Endive, radiccio, oakleaf, sorrel, and corn salad all make an interesting change from the lettuce we are used to seeing in salads.

Use plenty of color – red and yellow bell peppers, green snow peas, cherry tomatoes, and baby corn are all readily available.

Make up your own dressing with 3 tbsp olive oil, 1 tbsp whole grain mustard, 1 tbsp fresh chopped herbs, and plenty of salt and pepper. Place in a screw-topped jar and shake well to blend. Pour over the prepared salad and toss well to mix. Add the dressing just before serving, or the lettuce leaves will wilt and go soggy.

INDEX